The Sound Of Melanin

Written By

Kirk Nugent

"The People's Poet"

The Sound of Melanin
Written by:
Kirk Nugent

"The People's Poet"
Published by
Kirk Nugent Unlimited Global Enterprise LLC
Copyright 2020 Kirk Nugent Unlimited Global
Enterprise LLC
www.thesoundofmelanin.org
ISBN 978-0-9897513-2-2

Library of Congress Catalog Card Number:
00-090631

Dedication

This book is dedicated to my son, JuVon Kirkland Nugent. The person who gave me love unconditionally and taught me how to do the same. Son, always remember, if you don't have what you want, you're not committed to it one hundred percent. You will lose many false friends while chasing your dreams, but the ones that you gain in the process will be with you for life.

ALL is MIND. The Universe is Mental. Those seven words are the key to unlocking this Matrix that we call reality. You can only change the 'outside' from the 'inside'; therefore, if you don't go within, you will always go without.

Much Love,
Dad.

Acknowledgment

I want to express my gratitude to The Creator, thanks for the gift of words. This passion of mine has been a blessing and a curse; it has driven me to a life of extreme and uncompromised existence, the stories within me keep me restless until they're told. My undivided attention to the poetry within my soul has caused relationships that I wanted to see flourish to fail. Yet, I would have it no other way, this is my purpose, my reason for incarnating on such a complex planet within a seemingly unjust program that we call reality.

To all who have supported my dreams and my goals, my love for you will follow me into the next life and beyond. Special thanks to everyone who supported me and helped to make The Sound of Melanin a reality.

— Kirk Nugent

"The People's Poet"

CONTENTS

Introduction

I've found that human beings have the most difficult time digesting the truth. Americans especially, cannot deal with the truth when it comes to the issues of race and racism. The case of Jimmy "The Greek" is an ideal example. He said, "Blacks were bred to be bigger and stronger with a greater sense of endurance." Because of that statement, he was relieved of his position from a popular radio station. When in fact, what Jimmy spoke was the truth, unpopular yes, but the truth nonetheless. The fact remains that the biggest black slaves were bred with the strongest black slaves. We were bred like cattle for profit. However, Jimmy was ostracized and called a racist for speaking The Unpopular Truth. Why, in a so-called democratic society, a grown man is forced to bite his tongue is beyond me.

My goal with this book is to teach what I know to those who are unaware, so they might be able to rise above the perpetual mental enslavement that has plagued us for far too long. The truth doesn't always sit well with everyone, especially those who have systematically and habitually distorted, discounted, revised, and white-washed the truth. The 'Powers that used to be' hide the truth because they have always profited from keeping the masses in the dark.

When the truth does emerge, the forces of darkness shall rebel in the most violent, most devious, most diabolical manner one can imagine. Of course, the message that I'm sending via this book is unpopular. However, it is the truth (on a certain level of consciousness). It is contrary and in direct conflict with what the media have been spoon-feeding us for centuries. The initial reaction will be to attack the message, dismiss and discredit the messenger, then demonize and destroy the messenger, but regardless of how much it is distorted, the truth can never be killed.

Kirk Nugent

"The People's Poet"

The Unpopular Truth

If I speak The Unpopular Truth,
Does that make me a liar?
Because truth burns like flames,
And hypocrites try to put it out like wildfire.
Now, what if I told you that devils conspired,
To give you a Bible that would require,
Your submission to the atrocities
That slave masters transpired?
And that blue-eyed guy
That you so devoutly admire,
HE IS NOT THE MESSIAH.
The cat in the pulpit that tells you he requires
Ten percent of your salary
To save you from the hellfire,
He's an absolute liar.

Gain knowledge before you retire,
And you'll find that a secret order conspired,
To hide from you the knowledge that they've acquired,
So when I speak The Unpopular Truth,
You'll think that I'm a liar.

They tell you that you must suffer like the saints
To gain salvation,
Then take your money and build this capitalistic nation.
Have you thinking that being broke is a blessing,
Because the real truth you've been missing,
So it's not your religion, but hypocrisy I'm dissin'
When I say, "Fuck them and their Thanksgiving."

Catholicism and Christianity were not given to you
So that salvation you could win.
In fact, you've been worshiping a false doctrine.
False prophets gave you scriptures
Mixed with their pagan past.
You adopt it as your own, and the spell has been cast,
As they lead you through the gates of hell fast.
But if I speak The Unpopular Truth
I become an iconoclast.

Dealers of deceit have you thinking
That for Jesus you're making all this fuss,
But show me in your Bible,
Where Jesus celebrated Christmas.
Good Friday and Easter,
All traditions to honor false pagan Gods,
From Egyptian Baal to Babylonian Nimrod.

In the Ten Commandments,
The Bible warns not to bow to anyone
But the Almighty,
Yet the Pope has millions bowing
To a statue, that he calls Mary.
No one reads to see the contradictions,
And the lack of critical thinking is scary.

Scared to challenge traditions
Because pleasing a mortal man
Has become the central desire.
But if I speak The Unpopular Truth,
Does that make me a liar?

Black People yell, "Black Power, Black Power."
As they pump the Black Fist.
But I see too little activist and too many hypocrites.
We need to sit down and shut our mouths,
Was it not Negroes who voted Dinkins out
And Giuliani in?
Now they're begging this devil to repent for his sins.
It was blacks that sold Nat Turner
And Denmark Vesey out.
Sometimes it was at gunpoint
Harriet Tubman had to free
Slaves from the south.

Blacks executed Malcolm,
Because he was gaining too much clout.
Slave rebellion plots ended way before the attack,
Because most plots were sold out by blacks.

Long before we knew the words to,
"We Shall Overcome"
Blacks were the ones that sold out our freedom.
Sending tired blacks to martyrdom.
Sellouts informed overseers
That field negroes could become troublesome.
So now we march into the new millennium,
Not really free and still really dumb,
Failing to vote locally,
While filling these prisons.
'Black lives matter!' is what we holla
While refusing to leverage our dollar
With it's 1.2 trillion spending power.
We have the power, but we allow
Our economic situation to become dire
But if I speak the Unpopular Truth,
Does that make me a liar?

The media is the biggest proponent
Of racism on the scene,
In a fight, Tyson bit Holyfield,

The media reported
That he was a savage being,
Dehumanized him,
And compared him to the beast Wolverine.
A few weeks later,
Two white kids killed thirteen.
The media reported that
They were troubled teens.

They say, "It's not racism."
When white cops place our lives at stake,
But I never heard of a black cop
Killing a white kid by mistake.
Black girls get raped
And murdered every single day
With no airplay.
A couple of decades later,
And the media's still bugging about Jon Benet.
So don't tell me that against us
The media didn't conspire,
But if I speak the Unpopular Truth,
Does that make me a liar?

Here's an Unpopular Truth
That would cause white supremacy to disappear,
Every time I attempt to speak it

They say, "Nigger, don't you dare!"
Thomas Jefferson continually raped his slave
Sally Hemming's for years
But White historians reframed it
As a love affair.

Africans were civilized,
While Europeans were still living in fear.
Queen Victoria was called,
'The cleanest woman in England.'
Because she took a bath twice per year.
Bathing was an intricate part of African Islamic religions,
While Europeans emptied their dung in the yard,
This was their tradition.
Even when on their menstrual cycle,
Bathing for Europeans was vague,
Remember it was their filthiness,
That brought about The Black Plague.
Kings relieved themselves in the hallways of castles,
This was the norm for European Empires,
But if I speak the Unpopular Truth,
Does that make me a liar?

Some prefer to stay blind to the truth,
So they might as well take the "Blue Pill."
And live in The Matrix.

Let life bury them like a ton of bricks,
While they pray to their crucifix.
Devils politic, to transfix the Six, Six, Six
In the mix.

While diabolical minds stay creeping
Jokers haven't figured out that they've been sleeping.
Binary codes got your weakness exposed.
Sitting in front of your flat screen
With satellite dish and cable box,
Thinking you are watching a program,
While you're being programmed and watched.
Believing E-Z Pass was installed
So your travels can be swift,
When it's only another tool
For NSA to track you with.
ATM, cellphones, and credit cards locate you quick,
Email and text messages
Let them know who you politic with.
Your likes and comments on IG and Facebook
Let them know if you're a conservative,
Liberal or fundamentalist.
Everything's in place so that a Police State can benefit,
But I'm crazy when I say,
"America is on some Gestapo shit."

They've changed your Sabbath from
The 7th day to "SUN" day,
He came and saw natives, but
You celebrate Columbus Day.
Scratching lotto tickets hoping to change your luck,
Unaware that you've been ran amuck,
Programmed to self destruct,
With your scared conduct.

Remember our necks were broken on the gallows
In order to kill our hopes,
But fools don't know that ideas
Cannot be killed with ropes.
Twisting the truth to advance their greed,
But the biggest mistake they made
Was teaching me how to read.
Now things, that this poetic scene
Wouldn't contemplate or reckon,
I break down in four minutes and some seconds.
Not even bullets can silence me,
Because this new generation knows my poetry.
They wake up to see that against humanity
Devils did conspire,
So when I speak the Unpopular Truth,
They know that I AM no liar.

Programmed To Self-Destruct

Captain's Log: Stardate 2028.3

T minus ten and counting,

The negroes in America are drowning.

They were conceived in greed,

And raised by hypocrisy,

Now the American negro has met his destiny.

We distort their history,

Deprived and kept them impoverished.

We kill their dreams

Because where there is no vision, the people perish.

T minus nine and counting,

We've programmed the negroes to believe anything.

We tell them to be patient,

The Civil Rights bill is near,

This keeps the wool over their eyes

As we advance them to the rear.

In the media, let us parade them as thugs,

Hoods and society's misfits,

Give them an inferior education,

Then tell them they have a mental deficit.

T minus eight and holding steady,
The genocide is just about ready.
Give them welfare as a means of complacency,
They'll never know
That the price of greatness is responsibility.
Let us place a burden on the male
Far more than he could endure,
Now systematically,
That will destroy the family structure.

T minus seven and all is well,
The CIA has now introduced drugs
In the communities in which they dwell.
Have our officers slaughter
Their men in the early morning mist.
We'll use the jingle of money,
To kill the voice of justice.
If the negro enters our communities,
Keep him off-balance,
Make him a mental wreck,
Have our officers pull him over
For random spot checks.
Have them plant evidence
And break the negro's necks,
But in our community it is imperative

That our officers Serve and Protect.
This will ensure that when the negro
Speaks against us in tones that are inflammatory,
Even the so-called liberal whites
Will dismiss his ridiculous story.

T minus six, now let the supreme race be cleansed.
We'll use unemployment
To rip away at the very fabric of their existence.
Give them a few token laws,
Let them believe that these laws were God sent,
Deny them credit
And face them with perpetual disappointment.
Keep them discouraged,
Let them know at the end of the tunnel,
There is no light.
Control the media,
So the average white will not be sympathetic
To the negro's plight.

T minus five and we're almost done,
Refuse funding for schools,
But let us build more prisons.
HOUSTON WE HAVE A PROBLEM!
My Lord, the negroes are awakening,
Now they're saying that we are devilish.

Get the Secretary of Defense to counter the attack
By giving them a white Jesus to cherish.
Tell them that for their transgressions a white man
Sacrificed his very life,
And if they are well-behaved negroes,
With the said white man
In the afterlife, they will reside.
Tell them to love the people who abuse them,
And to pray for their oppressors to succeed.
Because with this type of conduct,
Oh, white Jesus is well pleased.

My Lord, there is no way
The negroes would believe such hogwash.
Of course, they will, they're negroes; with tiny brains.
They're intellectually inferior with limited
Capacity for critical thinking.
Just keep repeating the whole
Blond hair, blue eye, Lord and Savior Jesus story,
By nature, negroes are intellectually lethargic
For the truth, they will never search.
In a few generations, wild horses
Would not be able to drag them from the church.

Even if there is one among them that is wise enough
To know that there is no such thing as

Original sin from birth,
He still would not be able to convince them
That a benevolent white man did not surrender his life
So they could remain on Earth.
They would sooner ostracize such a one
And let his name be cursed,
Because negroes are intellectually insignificant
And far too ignorant to do their own research.
Sundays will be one great gigantic fashion show
Where negroes gather to repeat what they were told.
As long as they hold sacred the image of a white man
As their ultimate prize,
The church will always be the cornerstone in the
Foundation of their demise.

But in the meantime, assassinate
Their key black leaders one at a time,
This guarantees that the next generation falls in line.
We determine which negro they will support,
"Commander in Chief, nominate Clarence Thomas
To the Supreme Court."

For the White House; Ummm
Find us a smoking, well-spoken,
Non-provoking token.
One who encourages them to keep hoping,

While he's clearly joking
When he promises change, that they can believe in.
Let him keep them thoroughly entertained,
So metaphorically speaking
They'll never realize that they're bleeding.

Get us a character who will
Make the negroes feel at home,
But one who has no problem killing millions
Of brown folks with our precision military drones.
Make him charismatic and charming
Allow him humor, candor, and wit,
But when it comes to policies,
Ohhhhh, that negro boy better not
Deviate from the script.
We need him to kill willingly
Brown leaders like Muammar Gaddafi
Since he won't shut the fuck up
About returning his country to a
Gold-backed currency.

T minus four: Prepare to divide and conquer,
Impress upon the lighter negro
That he is better than the darker.
Mentally twist them in plain sight,
Even though every mass shooter has been white,

In that area, we will remain silent.
While we portray them as a
People that are prone to violence.
Have them believe that their vote
Will never make a difference.
Shake their confidence,
Question their intelligence,
Exploit their innocence,
Destroy their influence,
Deny their excellence, plant evidence.
Attack from every angle,
And the negro will have no defense.

T minus three and the negroes
Are not in the least terror-struck,
They're oblivious to the fact
That they've been programmed to self-destruct.

T minus two and the hour is at hand,
To completely remove the negro
From this promised land.
From the days of slavery,
His woman has always given him the courage
To endure even more.
Before we can destroy the negro,
He must identify with his woman

As a bitch or a whore.
Program him through his music,
As he laughs and dance,
He'll come to devalue his woman
Before he can awaken from this trance.
Financially encourage him to glorify
Murdering each other in his music.
Make it cool for him to spend time in prison,
Sort of like a rite of passage to catch a case.
But he dares not open his mouth in his music
And speak of harming any member
Of the white or Jewish race.

T minus one, now let us try this on for size,
We have the negro hypnotized,
Paralyzed,
Ostracized,
Supervised,
Disorganized,
Disenfranchised,
And by God we have them institutionalized.
In short, we have the negro neutralized.
Now give him superficial brand name clothing
And watch him cosign his financial demise.
Gather around gentlemen;
We have a dead body to eulogize.

The negro has neither political nor economic power,
The strong Black man
Has seen his final hour.
So on this chapter, let us close the door,
Gentlemen I'm proud to announce
That the threat of the American negro
IS NO MORE!

Mars 2039

You pollute the Earth with your political wars,
Now you have your satellite pointed at the stars
With the hopes of exploring Mars
But just who do you think you are?

And what if you went to Mars and saw Martians
But they didn't speak your language?
Would you call them savages?
And rob them of their heritage?
Commit them to a life of bondage?
And use their bodies as an experiment for syphilis?
Would you give them facilities
That were 'Separate but Equal'
And encourage them not to fuss?
Would you seat the green Martians
At the back of the Martian bus?

Upon your arrival
Would the Martians realize their greatest fears?
Would you march them across Mars on a 'Trail of Tears?'
Would you lynch the male Martians;

The ones you couldn't tame,
Whip the green Martians and change their names?
Or would you exploit them just for the sake of greed?
Would it be a crime for a Martian
To teach another Martian to read?
Would you abuse them for generations
You know, over a matter of time?
Would you make the color green
Synonymous with crime?

I know you would degrade them,
It doesn't take a genius to go figure,
You would probably start by saying,
"They look like little green niggas."
Would you treat them as livestock?
And raise the male to become breeders?
Would you orchestrate
The massacre of their Martian leaders?
And what if, there were a Martian King,
And a Martian X?
After you murder them,
Who would you slaughter next?
In the middle of the night
Would your Klansmen cut their throats?
Would they have to march for generations
Just for the right to vote?

And when you write your history books,
What would be your version?
Would you see the Martians as three-fifths of a person?
How many Martians would get a broken neck?
As your officers went out
To 'Serve & Protect?'

Their neighborhoods, would your bankers redline?
Setting interest rates that bleed out every dime.
And please keep in mind
That it would only be a matter of time
Before you establish a Martian school to prison pipeline.

When your cops murder them in the streets
And make sure that their brain matter splatter,
Would you be able to hear them
When they peacefully try to convince you,
That Green Lives Matter.
Would you set up a system to brainwash
Them in everything that they do?
Would you create a God for them to worship,
Who looked just like you?

And after you forcefully grab their land,
Would you tell them, 'This ain't no longer Mars,
This right here, is a part of Earth.

Shit, my grandfather been living here since birth
It was his toil that made this land now what it's worth.
And when the Martians try to sneak through your fences,
Seeking food to feed their faces,
Better opportunities for their babies,
Would you lock them in cages?
Telling them, 'This is about Law and Order
You green niggas need to start respecting our borders.'

And after you raped Mars, of every natural resource,
Next, would you send in your usual suspects?
First, the IMF to make sure that they're deep in debt,
Next, the CIA to get that destabilization
Program in full effect.
Vaccines laced with mercury to ensure birth defects,
Military occupation to keep them in check.
Ensure that the planet becomes an economic train wreck,
But do it gradually, so that the average
Martian doesn't even understand it.
So damn it,
Little Martian Janet can't even comprehend
That the destruction of her planet,
The CIA ran it.
Then would you say,
"Mars? Just another shit hole planet."

I'm just asking because I know what your
So-called explorations are worth.
Upon your arrival, you wiped cultures off the Earth.
So if you landed on Mars
The Martians would probably pray for death at birth,
So for the love of God
KEEP YOUR ASS ON EARTH.

40 Mill

Suckers spent 40 Mill to investigate Bill,
Because rumor has it, he lays pipe at will,
From Arkansas to Capitol Hill
So suckers spent 40 Mill.
While across from the White House
The homeless chill,
Junkies pop pills,
Senators shoot down civil rights bill
Cops violate us at will,
I mean shit is just ill,
But still,
Suckers spent 40 Mill
To see if Bill got skills.

40 Mill to see who Bill took in the sack,
'Cause rumor has it, he hit it from the back.
I heard he had two six-packs and just went black,
He was like, "Yo! Won't you let a President hit that?"
Now come over here and play on my sax
While I drop these sanctions on Iraq.
Forget about Abner Louima

And police crimes against blacks.
Forget the difference in sentence
Between cocaine and crack.
Forget the poor in the trailer park shack,
And forget the nines that these ten-year-olds now pack.
But let us spend 40 Mill to see who Bill took in the sack,
'Cause we need to know, did he hit it from the back?

40 Mill to see who's been making who moan,
40 Mill to see if Bill and Monica were ever alone,
And if they were, did Bill get blown?
What I'm asking is, "Did she play on his saxophone,
And make it grow into a trombone,
And if she did, did she speak into the microphone?"
40 Mill down the drain while the homeless moan,
40 Mill and you're sweating me
For a two grand student loan?
However you look at it, its 40 Mill
We could've used to achieve new milestones.

40 Mill to investigate all these theories,
Ask Hillary, and she'll tell you it's a conspiracy
To get her husband out the presidency.
And Bill said, "All these allegations I deny categorically.
In other words, I never touched Monica Lewinsky,
Only Hillary handles the jimbroski

So stop pitting her against me.
Besides I've never been this popular
Since I apologized for slavery
So fuck Ken Starr
And the player hating Republican party."

40 Mill, Y'all must be insane,
Spending 40 Mill to defame slick Willie's name
Playa hating because Bill got mad game.

40 Mill, now the story begins to unfold,
And Bill was like, "Damn! That fat bitch told."
He called Betty Curry and was like,
"Sweetheart hurry,
Drop what you are doing
And go see Monica forthwith,
And for God's sake try and recover all my gifts,
Cause she done broke the cup
From which me and Hillary sip,
And as far as Linda...ummm
Betty, that bitch is a TRIPP!"
CLICK!

He called Jesse Jackson
Because his situation seemed so unfair,
And said Rev. Jackson,

Could you please say a prayer?
"It is obvious, yet a pity
But you should've never, ever touched the titty.
Now, now, now, now, now, even though,
Even though you got caught
With your hand in the cookie jar,
Bill, I just love that thing you did with the cigar."

Bill said, "Jesse, Stop!
I can no longer concentrate,
My head is spinning so fast,
The only thought that enters my head
Is that they gonna impeach my ass.
Kick me out of the White House flat on my back,
Why is this happening to me Jesse?
I'M NOT BLACK!"

40 Mill to keep you distracted,
Now they've got you tuning in like fools,
While you're watching Bill,
They're cutting funding for public schools.
40 Mill to keep you focused
On Bill and Hillary's marital problems
Now y'all tell me what that gotta do
With the price of bread in Harlem?
40 Mill to make you say,

"Hell yeah, he jerked her."
Keep you distracted
While GM lays off another two thousand workers.

40 Mill to make you watch
As Congress brings him to his knees,
Keep you focused on the bullshit
While they ship our jobs overseas.
40 Mill to make you say,
"Hell yeah, Bill must pay."
Keep you blindfolded
While they execute Mumia in a few days.

It is 40 Mill hoping you'll be hypnotized
By their televised lies,
But I couldn't care less what Monica was doing
Between the Presidential thighs.
I'm not following all this litigation,
I don't care about Bill Clinton's frustration.
So don't let them distract you with their 40 Mill
And their stories about Bill
And his Oval office thrill,
And his DNA spill
Or any of the other bullshit
That don't mean nil.
Because the ones who program,

Program with skill,
They instill in your mind what they will,
So chill.
Before you end up
Like one of these domicile imbeciles,
Who was programmed on Capitol Hill,
With 40 MILL.

Ironic

You swept us from our beaches,
And dumped us on your sands
Black people in America
Were never welcomed on Ellis Island.
You changed our names to confuse our identity.
You deleted our religion and gave us Christianity.
You erased our contributions from your history text,
You change our thoughts, to one of divisiveness.
On your auction blocks, you placed us up for sale,
Now you want to tell us about your angry white male?

We educated ourselves, and now you see us as a threat,
Considering at one point teaching a black person
To read was a crime punishable by death.
Our schools are inferior,
While your kids are kept abreast
Because you view educating blacks as a conflict of interest.
You have no money for college grants
So we are denied our cap and gowns,
Yet you find forty-five thousand per year
To keep a brotha locked down.

You used religion trying to conceal your vanity,
Slaughter an entire race in the name of Christianity.
Remember, Manifest Destiny was the Red man's enemy.
You displaced us as a nation when
You stole us from Africa,
Now you want to tell us about some
Bullshit contract with America.
You said that physically we are unattractive
And deserve to return to the dust,
Yet every year you die of skin cancer trying to look like us.
You argue that we are repulsive
And the black man looks disfigured,
But Hollywood spends millions,
Trying to get her lips bigger.
You claim that we are inferior, your total opposite,
Yet you spend millions trying to look like us,
Sound like us, talk like us, walk like us,
Dress like us, dunk like us,
Ironic, isn't it?

Now you claim that we're a burden to this country,
And the welfare system is what sustains our lives,
But for each black on welfare, they're five poor whites.
You condemn cruelty around the world
As you bring it to the media's attention,

But lynching first occurred in America,
It was an American invention.
You claim that we're lazy as a people,
One of God's worst creation,
But step back in time, and you'll see,
It was black folks who built this nation.

During slavery, you lynched our men
And raped our women with a large mob,
A child lives what he learns, so yes America,
You taught us how to rape and rob.
You invented the rumor
That black men lusted after white women
For most of their days,
When in fact it was the white master,
Who sexually exploited his female slaves.
Historically, you stole from us,
Left us penniless and adrift,
Now at Christmas, you want me to tell my son
That some white man comes down the chimney
And brings him free gifts.
What's ironic is that negroes still fall for that bullshit.

Newt Gingrich shut the government down
Because for one flight
He was forced to sit at the back of the plane.
For years we were seated at the back of the bus

And our cries went in vain.
We marched for equal rights,
You watered us down fire hoses and
Treated us like filthy rags,
Now you want us to pledge allegiance
To a revised version of the Confederate flag.

You kept us out of boxing,
And the sport suffered a drought,
When we finally entered the ring,
We knocked your punk ass out.
What about when we came out singing?
You claimed it to be nothing but crap,
Except of course for all the pieces that Elvis jacked;
Now a great percentage of your teens watch MTV
And buy gangsta rap.

And if you think that's funny,
Umm...
Well, here's another paradox,
You claimed that our hair is nappy,
But you went and got dreadlocks.
You see, whatever we do,
You try to make a counterfeit,
Yet you despise us being black,
Ironic, isn't it?

Life Sentence

The crime I committed was unthinkable,
My attorney pleaded, "Insanity."
He said that mentally I was unstable.
I stood before the court;
Adorned in prison rags, I was filthy.
Has the jury reached a verdict?
"Yes, your honor, guilty!
Let us give him life, with no chance of parole."
But the judge said,
"No! That would destroy the body,
Let's destroy the soul."

The minute he read the sentence,
My eternal torment began,
They dropped me in twenty-first-century America
In the body of a Black man.
Now here I am a grown man
In a world that treats me like a child,
Wherever I went the cops harassed me
Saying that I fit some criminal's profile.
I try to walk the straight and narrow

But everyone treats me like a crook.
I tried to cross the street one day
And some old bitch clutched her pocketbook.
Gave me that look, as if I'm the one
That went across this country and
Everything the Natives owned, I took.

In the malls, security follows me
Cab drivers, up front, they wanted their fee.
On interviews, they filed my application,
Can't get a loan for my education.
In crimes, I'm first in the lineup,
To go to college, the Army insists that I sign up.
My civil rights they violate,
They left me depressed and desperate,
They say that I'm militant when I try to resist,
As they used my body as an experiment for syphilis.
Gave me inferior schools and inferior housing,
Their banks engage in redlining.
I can now sit in the front of the bus,
Yet I remain at the back of the line,
The color of my skin is synonymous with crime,
While racist judges are waiting to trade my life for time.

Their officers pull me over for random spot checks,
Formulate chokeholds to break my neck.

I was unarmed when their police gunned me down
In my town, with 41 shots.
Took the case to their courts and their justice system said
They saw nothing wrong with that.
In other words, nigger how dare you seek justice
Knowing goddamn well that you're black.
Damn near 400 years, and I'm still fighting for freedom,
Sitting in police precincts,
Pulling plungers out of my rectum.
Swallowing tears, watching law
Enforcement murder my sons,
On my person, planting cocaine and guns
Singing that good ole boy's anthem,
"Run nigger run!"

America watched as racist's cops beat Rodney King,
Bringing him to death's door within a degree,
Now you are asking me, to trust a justice system
That came back with a verdict of not guilty?
"He wouldn't stay down,"
And Amadou Diallo wouldn't go down,
America has always felt threatened
When the black man refuses to go down.
But I am here to stand in defiance of your racist alliance.
If this country was founded on a Christian legacy,
Then give me my place in hell,

Where we can all burn equally.

The soil of this land speaks for me, screams for me.
My tears and my blood dug deep into your soils
And the injustice it pondered.
Copulated with tormented souls of the Red man,
It changed the genetic makeup of your land.
Came back with a vindictive answer
Now, the very food you grow
Will eventually give you cancer.

My mere existence is a sin,
Every criminal has become my identical twin.
I'm an outcast like Rumpelstiltskin.
Lower than a snake in the grass,
Except I can't shed this black skin
I am surrounded by hypocrites
Claiming that they're born again,
As they lynch us time and time again.
But I'm tired of being hung by ropes on oaks,
At the hands of the good Christian folks.
Sick of being the butt of their corporate jokes
As they sip on Diet Cokes,
While puffing cigar smoke.
They act like they're making us some concessions,

But their sins don't get mentioned in their confessions.
I live in a state of fear and depression,
Until I became black
I never understood the psychology of oppression.
So how dare you try to act
As if all this injustice is in my mind,
When in my black skin, you've done no time.

Turned Tables

Dazed and confused,
Frustrated and fed up,
Numb by injustice,
Hopelessness won't even allow me to be pissed.
I'm tired of feeling like that one redneck in Montana,
Who keeps getting abducted by aliens,
Trying to explain his experience to a cynical nation.
No one understands my plight.
If only for one day I pray,
Not even to get back what they took,
I want just for a minute,
For the shoe to be on the other foot.

Snatch America by her blonde hair
And shove her in front
Of a full-length mirror, and scream,
"Look bitch! For once, open your eyes and look."
Yes, if only for one day
I would love to place the shoe on the other foot.

Get four big black bald brothers,

Give them nine millimeters and call them officers.
Then get one average white boy,
And to those racist cops,
He's just another cracker.
Trailer trash suspect,
That they're there to keep in check.
Chokehold reserved for white boys
To break his neck.
Whatever happens, I don't care,
Spare me the details.
Just make sure in the end
You've got me a dead white boy lying there.
41 shots later, your white son's lifeless body
Embraces the unforgiving ground,
And the four Black cops justify it by saying,
"Well, he wouldn't go down."

Let me see the tears flow
From his mother's rosy pink cheeks.
Let me hear her in anguish, reflect on his dreams.
Let me see her broken spirit,
Contemplate how her son could die
"He never bothered anybody, why God, why?"
Show me her faith in America,
When this country now changes the channel,
And turns a blind eye,

And Black politicians popping up
All over the News, saying,
"The shooting was justified."

Let me see her lips trembling,
But still trying to console his younger sister.
Let me gleefully listen to the news pundits
Saying, "It is unlikely that such a tragedy
Would've happened if he wasn't from a home
With an absentee father."
His family is weak from disbelief,
And emotionally fatigued,
While the four black cops on vacation in Jamaica
You know, they're on a paid leave.
Fighting to believe in a righteous black God,
Then have the black racist mayor get on TV,
Telling the victim's mom
That the officers were only doing their job.

Let me see you contemplate that shit.
Give you an opportunity
To get acquainted with the term,
Sick and tired of being tired and sick.

For once let me see
That white mother bent over in pain,

Let me see her take her son's body back to Sicily,
Israel or the Ukraine
And bury him in a pine box.
Let me indifferently watch,
As she fights back the knives
Slicing through her gut
But have no choice than in a racist black
Justice system to place her trust.
Let her watch as they move the trial
From Bridgeport, Connecticut
To Newark, New Jersey.
Have her wondering if God
Has lost his fucking mercy.
While cynical negroes snicker,
"It wasn't a crime, just a tragedy."
Hit her with that black conservative line,
"What you people need to do is focus
On all this white on white crime."

Let me with great indifference observe
Your community protesting,
Trying to appeal to my compassion
When I don't even see you people as humans.
Let me watch devils blame your innocent child
For getting himself killed.
This injustice makes you sick,

And after they screw you for the umpteenth time,
Listen to these callous negroes
Saying, "Well, we agree with the not guilty verdict."

Let me see you live that shit day after day
After day, after day, after day, after goddamn day
Then you'll understand
Why we ain't give a fuck if the killer was O.J.
But obviously, you chose not to learn,
So I pray for the day when the tables are turned.

Please understand that I get no pleasure
In the innocent slaughter of white youths,
I'm just sick of America acting
Like Ku Klux cops ain't the truth.
I don't want to see tears
Of hopelessness running down your cheeks,
Or your sons being slaughtered
Like hogs in the street.
But it seems like that's what it would take
For you to feel what I feel.
So just for once America,
Extend me some goddamn civility
And admit that my pain is real.

Amen

I'm sick of the hypocrisy.
It seems to me that the more devout they are,
The more they live to condemn me.
The more religious they are,
The more they live to judge me.
The more sanctified they are,
The more they vilify me.
The more impossible it is for them to see
That this poetry is my ministry.
And the closer they are to God,
The less likely it is for them to
See the God in me.

With conviction, I got on stage and confessed,
"My Past Keep Kicking My Ass."
And they were the first to blast,
To condemn me quick fast.
Quick to cause discord and crucify me with the sword
Because that's not the speech of one who loves the Lord.
So before my testimony can count,
They need to know the amount

Of my last tide,

Does my faith coincide

With the condemnation of gay pride.

Do I believe in the Trinity,

What are my religious affinity

Am I living in accord,

And when was the last time I was double dipped

Like a chocolate chip in the blood of the Lord.

Amen!

These hypocrites are so preoccupied

With their next life,

That if Jesus stood in front of them

They would not recognize the Christ.

I'm at a prison doing a speech, planting seeds

Making a difference to the ones in need, indeed.

Inmate walked up to me,

He said, "What up B?"

"I'm doing 25 to life, murder in the first degree."

He said, "The dude that I shot deserved to

Get his wig pushed back.

But before I had my seed, I was planning a killing spree.

I was tired of the church, the priest, and the hypocrisy."

"I was tired of that bitch ass nigga

In the robe that kept raping me.

Scared to death, cause he told me if I told
Jesus would straight barbeque my soul.
And although I've never been to the convent
I believed that when Jesus said,
'Suffer the little children to come unto me.'
Homeboy, that's not what the fuck he meant.
I was tired of my so-called Christian mom
Who wouldn't tell any of her Christian friends
That she had a grandson.
Because her son had that son
Out of wedlock, in short, fornication.
And Jesus wasn't down with that
Type of unbridle ejaculation.
In fact, if it ain't legit
Her Lord wasn't with that shit."

But what she failed to mention,
Was back then I was under some deep, dark depression.
Just to make it through the day I was
Sniffing all sorts of shit
I hated the world and every righteous motherfucker in it.
Ain't no minister had the nerve
To come on my turf and try to save me.
If I ain't come to church with his cover charge,
He ain't praying for me.
Hell was my only route,

Those were the words that came out of mom's mouth.
So I wanted to kill 'em all
And let the good Lord sort them out.
It's as if they think they won't have to pay
For the malicious shit that they say.
They're steady judging me, while preaching
About how forgiving their God is all day.
But I've got a full clip and an AK
To make sure they see that nigga today.

What mom failed to understand,
The formula she left out of the equation
Was that illegitimate child
Was my only legitimate salvation.
It was the only reason I didn't drop that
Clip in the AK and murdered her
And her entire congregation.
He said, 'Kirk, some people
Are so blinded by religion,
So god damn biblical,
That they can never recognize a modern-day miracle.
That bastard child that she wanted me to deny
Is the only reason she's alive.

But if you ain't holier than thou
Then you can't be counted among them.

And if this poem makes you uncomfortable
Then chances are, you are one of them.
These fools are so simple
That they believe if you're not in a building
Then you can't possibly be in a temple.

They're quick to condemn me
Because I use profanity in my poetry
Bitch, I told you that this shit is my ministry.
And truth be told, I've saved far more souls
In far less time,
Than you and your minister combined.
Because the people to whom
You're doing your so-called ministering,
Are already in the church,
Which means that they recognize that they're in sin.
They recognize the fact that something
Is wrong with the way they're living.

Me?
I spit to Bloods and Crips who don't give a shit.
Gangster chicks that only dip in stolen whips,
That eventually, they take to their man to strip.
They pack heat in their grip, extra clips with hollow tips,
Just in case some fool wants to trip.
Like American Express, they don't leave home without it.

I speak to emotionally cold,
Eight-year-olds who bust nines at the drop of a dime.
Oblivious to the concept of doing time,
Baby faced ten-year-olds who are just gorgeous
Courageous to the point of being contagious,
Done dismiss the thought of living past Christmas
So God forbid they've got some beef with you
They're ridiculous with their focus.
They pack enough ammo
To make a whole precinct nervous,
And the church ain't nothing but a building
For your funeral service.

They're proud to be called a pimp.
The sheep; they live to devour.
Because exploiting the weak makes them strong
And in the streets, it's all about power.
But I get up in their head
With this so-called profane poetic bullshit,
And because I speak the language of the street
They don't dismiss it as foolishness.
Fact is, they're kind of cool with it
So I take them to school with it,
Give them paradigm shifts
And allow them to fool with it.

However, these are no ordinary skeptics.

They're not big on trust

So it is imperative that I must

Plant my knowledge more tactfully than Henry Kissinger.

I'm feeding the souls of what you call scavengers,

Who incidentally happen to be smart enough

To extract the message without

Condemning the messenger.

So while you're in the church dancing

About how the Holy Ghost is filling you,

I'm in the streets trying to reach these little boys

Who wouldn't give a fuck about killing you.

And if I ask you to see the God in these kids, you can't

But unlike yours, my message is perfect for

Those of us who aren't.

That's why I show them that emotions are like a gun

And only the weak allow someone else to pull their trigger,

Because the one who holds the gun

Suffers the consequences forever.

I introduce them to Sun Tzu and The Art of War

Show them how that concept relates to the street

And watch their jaw drop in awe.

Intellect homeboy, that's the currency of the hour

Collect enough chips and watch

Your statue begin to tower.
And regarding the term, 'pimp,'
That's just an acronym for
Persuasive Individual Managing Power.
So if you've got to use force
To get someone to be submissive
It means you've got no power,
And you damn sure ain't persuasive.
Force should never be your only recourse
That's a slave master's mentality
And wherever there's a slave master
There's a slave waiting to cause mutiny.

I watch the seeds that I plant begin to take hold
Souls that were cold begin to warm and make a difference
Instead of acting out of callousness,
They now act out of conscience.
True, they're not living in a state of bliss
But at the same time, there's an absence of malice.
I see in their eyes, something I've never seen before
A flicker of hope, a shedding of resentment
Still strapped but now willing to
Walk away from an argument.
No longer hell-bent, by God, they're willing to relent
Because they understand that
Behind every choice lies a consequence.

I see Christ in them, as their torment become absent.

Their spirit has never been this present.

So, of course, my poetry you resent

Because it represents

Another soul being saved

Without paying your bitch ass ten percent.

Amen!

The Psychology of Oppression

Until the story of the hunt is told by the lion,
The tale of the hunt will always glorify the hunter.
— African Proverb

When the first slave ships arrived on the shores of America,
The Africans who disembarked those ships,
Psychologically speaking, they were like a child.
They were like a child because
They were told what time to eat,
What time to sleep, where to be,
And when to be there.
They had no free will to exercise,
And were severely punished if
They made any attempts to do otherwise.
So indeed they were like a child;
A severely abused, dazed, and confused,
Trauma-induced child.
America was the adult,
The child molesting, murdering, raping,
Barbaric, satanic, demonic, Christian adult.
So from initial contact to this day,

This land was designed to kill the African.
From Uncle Sam, to the Klu Klux Klan,
J. Edgar Hoover with the Feds at his command.
So even down to the very law of the land,
It was designed to ensure that
Africans did not take a defiant stand.

So like I said, psychologically speaking, we were children.
But the children that were shipped to the West Indies
Were exceptionally wild, a rebellious bunch.
These were not the type of kids
Who you were going to get
To willingly hop, skip, and jump.
To work all day for little or no lunch,
Or some goddamn Captain Crunch.
No, not without introducing your head
To some type of trauma that was blunt.

Naw, you see, these kids packed a punch.
Especially those dropped off in the islands of Jamaica
And Haiti aka Saint Dominique,
Where the situation seemed exceptionally
Bleak for the meek.
But these Africans being unique, did not believe in defeat.
They were not yet acquainted with the white man's Bible
Encouraging them to turn the other cheek.

Return the oppressor's evil with good deeds,
And you'll be rewarded after Jesus
Wake you from your sleep.
Naw, these Africans were lions, not sheep.

Their ancestors spoke to them
Through the mystique of the drumbeat.
And they had the physique that could unleash
A biscuit and a two-piece by rocking any mouthpiece.
In a heartbeat, they could put their oppressors to sleep,
With blade in hand, one sweeping leap
Left the overseers six-foot deep.
Snap their spines until their heads
Touched the back of their feet,
These brothers invented the idea of making ends meet.
They were not the type of Africans to hold their peace,
These were tribal warriors who would behead you
And leave your body as a conversation piece,
Watch your village burn while
They made preparations for a feast.
Capeesh?

The English and the French soldiers had their rifles
And they felt particularly brave
But these African brothers and sisters were unfazed.
They ain't used to being no slave,

They ain't accustomed to being well behaved.
They bout to be up in Mr. Charlie's face like aftershave
Leave him dazed while they set this bitch ablaze.

You see, back then we were
In tune with our spiritual practices,
We had a knack for this,
We weren't actors and actresses
Making money on our backs on mattresses.
Naw, we studied manuscripts like shopping lists,
That's how the various tribes coexist.
They navigated the jungle at a fever pitch,
Moving so silently, so deadly, so swift.
They could slit your throat before you could even twitch,
And when your friends found your body
They would think that the Matrix
Had a glitch in that bitch.

This knowledge was handed down
From generation to generation,
It was the secret to our salvation.
We mapped our location by the stars
And the songs we sang;
Alerted the other tribes that it was time for war.
When all the heavenly bodies became aligned
We knew It would be our time to shine.

Through the wisdom of
Our divine Ancestors,
They gave us rituals to keep us sane,
Rituals to break any chain,
Rituals to bring the pain,
Rituals to make you act right,
Like Bruce Lee when he ran up on Chuck Norris,
You see back in the day; we didn't go to the trunk,
We went to the forest.
So our Rights of Passage we faithfully sought
Because it prepared us for whatever
Opposition our enemies brought.

So one night, when the ancestors
Said that the timing was right,
Guided only by the moonlight, the will to fight,
The knowledge that freedom was our birthright,
And the fact that the ancestors gave the green light.
One of our great spiritual warriors by the name Boukman
Set sail from Jamaica towards the northeast,
To meet with the voodoo priests of Saint Dominique.
His mission was simple: Free his people by
Slaughtering the Beast.
You see, back then, 'No Justice, no peace.'
Wasn't just an empty phrase
That sell-out negroes gave the masses

To chant in order to put liberal minds at ease.

This brother was given the name of Boukman

Because he was well-read and well versed

In the ways of our ancestors and our culture.

He was a guardian against colonizing vultures.

Unlike the negroes of today,

Boukman had knowledge of self

He was not a slave, and he understood that,

If Boukman were alive today,

He could not be bought with an NFL contract.

Because of his deeds, it was illegal

For blacks to learn how to read.

This story is not in your history books

Because Boukman's courage might just reach you.

Beseech and teach you.

It's their job to mislead you

But it's your job to connect the dots my people.

Boukman got with the spiritual elders of Haiti,

And they meditated and prayed

To their African Gods and their African ancestors,

Until they fell into a trance.

Then they started doing that dance,

That dance that only our hips can rock

That dance that only our DNA can unlock,

That dance that they thought they could stop.

But they couldn't hold us with chains and padlocks
Because we were warlocks with dreadlocks
Who knew how to pop-lock.
That dance when heard by our enemies,
They subconsciously knew they were about to get dropped
That dance that gave us visions of their burial plots,
Letting us know that it was time to clean clocks.

Long before that hour,
We understood the power of our Melanin
And so we danced in awe.
Singing songs of freedom,
Tribal members gathered from near and far
That night they dropped more than 32 bars,
Dancing under the cover of night,
Channeling the Gods of War
Lifted by the smoke from their ganja cigars.
The lightning and thunder became the electric guitar
And ancestors replenished our spiritual reservoirs.
They became one with every planet,
Every moon, every quasar,
You see back then, we actually knew
What it meant to be Dancing with the Stars.

The shamen of the tribes
Slaughtered the fatted calf and offered the blood

As libation to the Gods of their ancestors.
Yes, they sacrificed an animal
And offered the blood as a libation,
Just like you've read in the Old Testament
When any of the great men
Wanted God to be on the battlefield with them,
They sacrificed an animal to gain the blessing.
But when you do it for your empowerment,
It's voodoo; it's satanic, it's evil,
Yes, they gave you their religion
To disconnect you
From your power my people.

Back then on those sugar plantations,
The slaves were worked until their muscles
Detached from their bones,
They were being worked to death if need be.
So no one thought black folks were lazy
Until we stopped working for free.
You see, these devils had
Neither conscience nor empathy.
So when Boukman prayed to his ancestors,
They said, 'Black man you come
From a lineage of mighty warriors,
If you want your freedom,
You're gonna have to fight for it.'

Get it?
If you want your freedom,
You're gonna have to fight for it.
Not march for it,
Not protest for it,
Not take a knee for it,
Not any of the nonsensical things that we now do,
The only person that you need to convince
That your life matters is you.

But also your dignity matters,
Because at one point our resolve was made of steel,
Now we're being bought and sold
For movie, record, and sneaker deals.
Your word matters and your integrity matters,
But I don't think you're ready to fight for your freedom,
You just want to shine on social media with that,
'My life is so awesome' chatter,
Because most importantly,
Your spending habits matter.
If you want to hit the Capitalistic Beast in its heart,
Then fight with your dollars; that's where you start.
Recognize your value.
The NFL doesn't care about you,
Yet they couldn't make a dime without you.

Yet they make beaucoup dollars off of you,
Black folks are so afraid
That they might get the Kapernick fade,
So they fail to realize in this day and age
With the bank that they make,
They could leave this whole system shook
Just by redirecting the dollars in their pocketbooks.
But white supremacy has convinced you
To look in the mirror and be displeased.
My people, you are beautiful.
If only those words you would believe
Then you would stop spending a half a trillion per year
With people who don't give a fuck about you
On perms and hair weaves.
But you ain't ready for this level of truth
So let me get back to Boukman
And the French/Haitian dispute.
Let me get back to when black folks
Were not compromised, but rather resolute.

So our God told Boukman
That when you step on to that battlefield,
We, your ancestors, by your side will stand,
We will lay waste to the enemy,
And they will flee this land.
You're black, and you're bold,

You're magical, and you're strong.
You see, back then we prayed to a different God
A God who understood the urgency of our situation,
A God who heard our cry and was responsive to our needs.
A God who knew how to make our enemies bleed,
Indeed we knew a God who would destroy their seeds
And scatter them like tumbleweed.
Similar to the Native Americans,
We were not familiar with the white man's God.
This God who for over 400 fucking years
Have been telling us
To put ten percent in the plate, and wait.
We were not familiar with this new God
Who allowed enemies to walk into our place of worship
And murder us without any retribution.
Have law enforcement take our killers to Burger King,
Naw, our God didn't have that
Bitch ass type of constitution.

We were intimately, and intricately connected to our God,
We didn't need a book to receive a Word.
The slave praying to the slave master's God,
Is one of the dumbest thing I've ever heard.
The Prison Industrial Complex is a topic
You've never heard addressed
By any white televangelist

Because they know that slavery never died,
They just rebranded it.

J. Edgar Hoover, through CoinTelPro
Destroyed every system and every institution
That empowered Black folks as such
But he left the black church,
In the black community, untouched.
Because he knew that having
A black man bow to a white God;
That psychological damage was more than enough.
And if one negro resisted,
There would be ten thousand believers
To put him back in line.
So thank you very much.
Once you've brainwashed the massive
They will kill any influx of knowledge.

So after the ancestors gave the green light,
We went to war with our Gods by our side.
And from 1791 to 1803,
We went about putting an end to our oppression,
Whopping ass in high definition,
Putting the French army out of commission.
We had them squirming in the fetal position
When they encountered the beauty

Of this old-time religion.
Under the leadership of a runaway slave
By the name of Toussaint L'Overture
It was like possessed Jehovah Witness'
Going out to explore,
The Haitians delivered a most
Unmerciful flogging, door to door.
A machete to the head was how they built rapport,
Wasn't no HBO, but white folks
Were feeling quite insecure.
A two by four planted inside a French
Soldier's skull was the new decor,
It was nothing but blood and gore
As they fled to their ships and rowed offshore.
The Haitians not only drove the French out of their land,
Had them fools fleeing through the jungle like Tarzan.
But they also went next door to whop ass some more
They ran up on the Spanish slave
Owners in Santo Domingo,
Today it is known as the Dominican Republic,
And those Haitians took a stand.
Appearing out of nowhere like the Invisible man
Clubbing the Spaniards to death like Captain Caveman.
It's like they were channeling Wu-Tang
When they pulled out the chitty-chitty bang bang
And started reducing life span

Like when Django went to Candyland.
Over the next several months
They whopped ass on an installment plan,
Leaving the slave owners looking like Raggedy Ann.
They did not stop until they freed the entire nation,
And ironically today,
Dominicans because they're lighter-skinned
Believe that they're better than Haitians.
Because of their complexion and their programming,
They've grown ignorant and vain,
Yet, had it not been for the Haitians,
Dominicans would still be in chains.

Now speaking of the French and Spanish,
They were heavily armed and better equipped
And today when they talk about their defeat,
They will admit that, indeed, it was tragic.
But the wisest among them knew,
That in actuality, it was Black Magic.

Now once word got back to the 13 colonies
That the Africans in the West Indies got bold,
That they did some spiritual rituals and went rogue.
Splitting the French throats before they could reload,
Club to the head made sure it explodes
Gutting them like fish, leaving their intestines exposed.

Virginia passed what would become
Known as the Slave Codes,
To ensure their system of white supremacy
And guarantee that for generations
They would still be whistling Dixie,
While ensuring that we would be
Dealt with brutality and inhumanity
They declared that all enslaved Africans
Must be converted to Christianity.

I'm a give you a minute to let that marinate,
Because that one action sealed our fate.
You see, you became a Christian
Because your mother was a Christian.
And your mother became a Christian
Because your grandmother was a Christian.
And your grandmother became a Christian
Because her grandmother was a Christian.
But the dot that you failed to connect is that,
That last grandmother that I mentioned,
She was illiterate.
So you're making a decision
On a God to run your life,
Based on the information that you received
From someone who could neither read nor write.

There was a deep sense of urgency
To see African spirituality meet its demise,
Oh, these devils were wickedly wise.
Practicing our religion was strictly forbidden
Get caught, and you were taken by surprise
Penalized by being burned alive,
Screaming in agony in front of young,
Terrified black eyes.
They made sure we were traumatized
So that our minds could be sterilized.
Eventually, we forgot the names of our Gods
In order to survive,
Wasn't long before the Bible became true lies
And we were told for our wretchedness,
A white man was crucified,
Gave us an image to worship
Of blonde hair and blue eyes.
Took away all the images of the Black deity,
And the only scripture we ever heard from the Pastor,
Was slaves obey your masters,
With respect and fear,
Just as you would obey Jesus Christ.
You can find that bullshit scripture
In Ephesians six, verse five.

Black Africans being empowered by

Black African deity is dangerous,
They said, give them a God that looks just like us.
Greek scholars went to Egypt
And studied our ancient manuscripts,
Isis and her son Horus were converted
To Mary and Jesus for simplicity.
They marveled at our knowledge,
While repackaging our story under their ethnicity.
The black man has been lost,
Ever since the white man
Turned his ankh into a cross.
And to this day the negro prays
To a blonde hair, blue-eyed God
Asking to be freed from
A blonde hair, blue-eyed devil.
You refuse to see plainly,
That the ones who gave you
Your religion are shady,
They still mad at Haiti.
We live in a so-called Christian country
With no Christ-like tendencies.
They turn a blind eye to the inhumanity,
Discarding the poor is their pedigree,
Just think about it, and you will clearly see
That the only Devil black folks have ever known
Is the system of white supremacy.

They said, while by force,
We will aggressively take whatever we want,
Teach the negroes to wait upon the Lord.
While we build generational wealth
On the backs of their sacrifice,
While we teach the negro
That their reward is in the next life.
Teach the negro the virtues of self-sacrifice,
Teach the negro that everything will be all right
Once they die and go be with White Christ.
Tell the negro that his reward is in heaven,
Tell him to desire a good life,
And wealth is of the devil.
Tell him, blessed is he
Who lives below the poverty level,
Tell him to lay down his life,
Because a greater love hath no man.
But for us white folks, here's the plan
Let us own all the stocks, the bonds, the oil,
The water, the buildings, the land,
The birth certificate and the straw man.

And today, if you meet a white person who's a Christian,
They're going to try and convert you to Christianity.
And you might say, well that's just what Christians do

Bring as many souls to Christ,
Have a spiritual breakthrough.
But how come they never try to convert the Jew?
My negro, it's just you.
Because white supremacy
Will always set the precedence
To make sure that your power
Comes from a God who is impotent.
And as logical as my argument is,
For the average negro cognitive dissonance
Will allow them to dismiss me swiftly.
They will argue for the Bible and all its mysteries,
But what they will never do
Is go and research their history.
These, 'I've read one book, and that's all I need.'
Johnny come lately
Will never take the time to emancipate
Themselves from mental slavery.

Amun-Ra and Imhotep are not just characters
That Hollywood pulled out of the blue.
And even though they know that you're asleep
And clueless like Scooby-Doo
They couldn't risk you having a breakthrough
As you did back in Timbuktu.
So in 2016 Hollywood spent millions on a switcheroo

Trying to solidify that point of view.
Trying to convince you that
The Gods Of Egypt didn't look anything like you.
Not true.

However, what these ignorant negroes cannot argue
Is that whenever the Klu Klux cops lynch your sons,
The God of the oppressor makes sure
That they suffer no judicial price.
Whenever the cops murder your Tamir Rice,
Your Eric Garner,
Your Amadou Diallo,
Your Sean Bell,
Your Sandra Bland,
Your Terence Crutcher,
Your Mike Brown,
Your Corey Jones,
Your Kevin Matthews,
Your Michael Noel,
Your Leroy Browning,
Your Philando Castile,
Your Nathaniel Pickett,
Their God make goddamn sure,
No matter how wicked,
That they're never prosecuted,
Or held in prison for one single day.

Then the same God tells you
To hold candlelight vigils and pray,
The same God, tells you the same thing
He's told you for 400 years,
He tells you to wait.
He says the same thing he always says,
'Justice is coming; just not today.'
Be patient, and while you're being patient
He needs more tithes and offerings,
And could put a little something
On the building fund for him.
Don't be coming up short with the ends,
It's 2020, and the Lord don't want to see
Pastor pushing no 2019 Benz.
How blind do you have to be
Not to see the fallacy?
That the slave master's God
Will never deliver you
Out of the hands of White Supremacy.

Every time a racist cop slaughter
Your sons and daughters,
You come seeking justice,
Praying for a court order,
But instead, you're told, be patient.
We live in a democracy,

And everyone is equal under the law,
The system is just not perfect.
You go home, and you accept it,
But you stand corrected,
You see, we live in a
System of white supremacy
That has been perfected.

You go overseas and die in their wars,
Return riddled with trauma and battle scars,
And they'll tell you,
'You knew what the fuck you signed up for.'
That's about as empathetic as
You're going to get out of that chatter,
So why are you in the streets
Trying to convince these people
That Black lives matter?
The best thing you can do is go home,
And decide to do better.
Read a book and unlock your mind
From the program that now festers,
That's the very least you could do
To honor your ancestors.

And If you knew the power
And the magic of your Melanin

You would **NEVER** wear a weave
Or bleach your black skin.

Every institution that has ever stood
For any real advancement of black folks,
Have been targeted,
And destroyed without a hitch.
Infiltrated and scrambled in the mix,
Blacklisted like the apocalypse,
Labeled terrorists until they
Simply cease and desist,
Harrassed until they no longer exist.
Today If you peacefully protest police brutality,
The **FBI** labels you a 'Black Extremist.'
The **FEDS** provides the transcript
And the courts make sure
It ain't no slap on the wrist.
If the church were contributing
To black folks progress
It would not be allowed to exist.
Everything of substance including reading,
Language, culture, and spiritual practices
Were taken away from the slave,
Yet Christianity was allowed, those are the facts,
And here we are in 2020,
And you're not bright enough to ask yourselves,

"Why is that?"

Black neighborhoods have churches, liquor stores,
Fried chicken joints, and strip clubs
On just about every street,
That's everything you need
To keep the negro docile and asleep.
This system of white supremacy
Delivers nothing but pain and evil,
Your brain is the vein,
Christianity is the heroin,
And the church is the needle.
I need you to start
Connecting the dots my people.
Stop dismissing information that
You have not researched as hogwash.
The reason you don't know that
You've been lied to,
Conditioned and brainwashed,
Is because you've been lied to,
Conditioned and brainwashed.

Without a doubt, there are some in the audience
That finds it a blessing
That we've come to the end of this lesson.
And for those who can put aside

Ignorance and cognitive dissonance,
The programming about the God
That you were told to romance,
Before this poem made
Something in your gut started sinking.
I've got a question,
A question that doesn't even require critical thinking.
Just plain old common sense,
Ponder at your own expense.

The question is:
Why would a person
Who has historically
Sold you,
Lynched you,
Murdered you,
Raped and enslaved you,
Burned you alive,
Infected you with syphilis,
Plant evidence and imprison you,
Jailed you disproportionately.
In Flint, poisoned your water,
Burn all of your homes and business
To the ground in Tulsa, Oklahoma.
Bombed you in Philadelphia
When you were more peaceful than him,

Murder you at traffic stops,
And move out of the neighborhood
Whenever you move in.
Why would this person give you a religion,
A roadmap that will ensure you can spend
All of eternity in paradise with him?
Why would he do that,
When he finds the very sight
Of you here on Earth sickening?
Are you that naive to believe
That someone who has spent his entire existence
Trying to destroy you,
Would introduce you to a God,
Who could actually save you?

I Believe

I never believed in the tooth fairy,
Hardy Boys or Nancy Drew mysteries.
I never believed in the Bogeyman,
And on December 25,
Santa Claus was not involved in my plans.
I had no faith in the Genie in the bottle,
And sometimes I question the validity
Of this book that you call, 'The Gospel.'

And being that I'm living in America,
My lucky diamond pinky horseshoe ring,
Could never cover the sins of my skin
So in short, I don't believe in a lot of things.
And I damn sure don't subscribe to the hypocrisy,
But follow me when I say I believe in poetry,
Persistence, passion,
Tailoring my life in my very own fashion.
I never believed in accepting the leaves or the fruits,
Instead, I want to dig up the tree and examine the roots.
But I do believe in my right to command this stage
And spit the 'Unpopular Truth.'

I believe that nothing in this world can ever deter me,
I believe that one man with courage is a majority.
I believe in letting the cat out of the bag,
Spilling the beans,
Kicking the real deal Holyfield
So don't invite me to the mic
If you don't want me to keep it real.

I get raised eyebrows from Conservatives,
When I say that the Founding Fathers were hypocrites,
And Thomas Jefferson was a rapist.
They look at me as if what I'm saying
Is some hidden mystery,
But don't hate me, hate your history.
As a matter of fact, I'll say it again,
They were bitch-ass hypocrites,
"All men are created equal," but I'm three fifths?
Good ole' massa Jefferson, a predator in the midst.
Congressman, Statesman, rapist.

They've been lying to you from the cradle to the grave,
When have you ever heard of a slave master
Having a love affair with a slave?
How you gonna accept the fallacy that they gave?
Do you not understand the definition of the word slave?

It means she could not oppose any
Advances that he made,
It means that she could not deny any orders that he gave,
It means she had no choice in the matter,
It means if she resisted her eyes would grow blacker,
As he back slaps her, attack her,
Whiplash, and unwrap her.
Talk to me like I'm grown and stop being rude,
Do you believe at any point Sally Hemmings
Could've said, "Massa Jefferson,
Tonight I just ain't in the mood."

Please, he would've broken her down like a Rubix cube,
Tossed her up like undigested food.
Get her acquainted with the heel of his boot.
With a closed fist, he would've split
Her lips and removed a tooth.
You know...the typical white supremacist foreplay
To get black women in the mood.
Wrap her up like a Subway sandwich
He owned slaves,
So we know the bastard was into bondage.
He probably would've taken a pitchfork
To the back of her head
Like he was fending off some danger,
Kicked her legs apart and rode her like the Lone Ranger.

Smacked her around as he rearranged her,
Threaten to take her to the auction
Blocks and exchange her,
Brag to the other Senators
About how he's gonna break her.
Probably cocked his shotgun in her mouth
So he could get off on her fear,
Call me pragmatic but that shit
Don't sound like no love affair.

And she survived...
She survived because I don't believe
That the human spirit can ever be outdone,
I don't believe NYPD thought Diallo had a gun.
I never believed that with Giuliani as mayor
We would get justice in the long run,
And obviously, I don't believe in biting my tongue.

However, I do question the hypocrisy
Of these voters who chime,
"How could God allow our kids
To be slaughtered in Columbine?
Where was He, isn't this His Universe
And doesn't He rule?"
But when will they learn,
This is America, and God isn't allowed in schools.

So there, deal with that unpopular fact,
Maybe that's why no one got shot in the parking lot.
"How about that Mr. Fung?"

I believe America has a vested interest
In giving my son a gun,
I believe they're making billions
From pouring nicotine into his lungs
No longer from trees,
But from legislative branches, we're being hung.
I believe the racial divide has only just begun,
Because if they can keep everyone focused
On the bitterness of the past,
You'll be distracted long enough
For them to eradicate the middle class
And when you wake up,
It will only be the super-rich
And your racist broke ass.

But I believe in our ability to succeed,
And I believe in my right to make this pen bleed.
I believe in living on my terms,
Not living so that mommy and daddy can be fulfilled.
I believe in poetry, passion, and the power of the will.
I believe that persistence is far more important than skills
But I damn sure don't believe in no diet pills.

I don't believe that women
Should try and fit into some prime time mold
Given to them by some fat, ugly, beer belly media mogul.
Some cigar-puffing, hair losing,
Child-molesting, sex trafficking, middle age joker,
Some mediocre, chain smoker, porn broker.
Naw, I believe that women should be thick,
With thick thighs and thick hips
And a big curvaceous, bodacious behind
That makes my neck snap every time they walk.
After all, meat is for the man; bones are for the dogs.

I don't believe in taking myself too seriously,
I've learned to laugh at life's little jokes,
I believe that J-O-B be an acronym
For Journey Of the Broke.
Therefore, if you're unhappy with your job,
You should quit.
But first, call out sick,
Use all your sick days and vacation time fast,
Then tell the boss,
"You can kiss my narrow,
Black, Jamaican stretch mark covered ass."

I believe in being frank, I believe in being candid.

I believe that if you have something to say
Then get it off your chest dude.
I believe that you get ulcers not from what you eat
But from what's eating you.
I believe that nothing in this world is worth stressing me,
I believe that the right woman brings out the best in me.
Ain't nothing in this world,
Like a woman who turns me on mentally,
A friendship that grows to love eventually
I believe that's just God's way of blessing me.

I believe that character, not skin, determines the man,
I believe that racism is a fear of what we don't understand.
I believe that most lawmakers are insecure racist jerks
I believe in equal pay for equal work.
Because it really doesn't make any sense that
For every dollar a man earns, a woman only gets 75 cents.
If a good woman is the backbone of every strong man
Then the least we can do for our mothers and daughters,
Is to give them their goddamn quarter.

I believe that we need to look
A little deeper below the surface,
Because blacks and whites
Share the same common interest.
We both desire love, to feel wanted and needed,

But it's in the interest of a few to keep us divided.
Give us a preoccupation with color,
While they rape healthcare, leave us both in the gutter.
Tax your shelter so don't trust them with your funds,
Bleed social security and control the guns.
If it wasn't for George W,
These S and L scandals wouldn't be there to trouble you.
Strip you of your dough as they rape Medicare and HMO
But before you can focus and
Realize who is the real foe
They ask:
"Aren't you sick of these complaining-ass negroes?"
Keep the divisiveness fresh in your head
While they have you on your financial deathbed.

I believe the media's job is to manipulate, not to inform,
I believe that white sheets have been replaced
With blue uniforms,
I believe nooses have been replaced with nines
And Klan members wear uniforms and badges at times.
I believe in Karma,
I believe that you will repay the debts of your sin,
I believe that the man who won't stand convicted
In his beliefs will eventually fall for anything.
But I don't believe in their illusion of inclusion,
Instead, I believe in the science of noncompliance,

Defiance, self-reliance, and strategic alliance.

So obviously, I believe in a lot of things,
But most of all, I believe in the power within.
I believe in poetry, persistence,
And living life with passion.
I believe in chasing impossible dreams because
Fear always buckle in the presence of action.
I believe that we're the cause of our own unhappiness,
I believe there's so much inside of us
That we haven't tapped yet.
I believe in experiencing life through every single breath.
I believe that there is greatness
In each and every one of you
And I challenge you, not to settle for anything less.
That's what I believe.

Gangsters R US

I've heard these so-called rappers on their
CDs and MP3s decree
That a cat like me could never understand
The degree of how dangerous they could be.
They said, 'Yo B, you best not find the audacity,
To provoke us to wrath,
Because a cat like you lack the capacity,
And the tenacity to deal with the
Bloodbath and the aftermath.
Because once the flame gets sparked,
Then the guns gots to bark,
And for mad motherfuckers shit gone get dark.
I'm talking laying on the sidewalk covered in white sheet,
Outlined in chalk type dark.

The first sign of beef and we handle our business.
We've got a sickness that makes us
Clap back with a quickness
The MAC-10 don't leave no witness.
So you can go ahead and dis' this
And watch your entire clique get dismissed.

We bring it like Baghdad up in this bitch
Poet niggah; you don't want none of this.
Cause when we come thru in the stolen Jag,
We'll clean you up like a Stridex Pad
Leaving nothing but body bags and toe tags
CSI be looking at your body like, "Daaaag.
He made somebody mad."
While trying to explain to your grandad
How the fuck you became a hashtag.
So you better wish upon a
Dope beat that this rap shit work,
Before we get lit, hit the streets,
Cause you grief by putting in work.
We the Al Capones of Don Corleones
Of this urban war zone.
So be careful what you say and
Even more careful what you do
Before me and my crew come through
And lay you out like the flu.
Run up on you
And make it do what it do.
When we hit you with that one, two.
Leave you mad drowsy,
Have you thinking we Amanda Nunes
And you're Ronda Rousey.
Got a Magic 8 ball?

You better ask it
Don't piss us off, that's what the task is.
Cause the gasket will put you in a casket,
Have your moms receiving floral baskets.
I told you, when it's time to scold you,
I don't keep it holstered.
Burner always in hand,
Toast you like the gingerbread man
Poet niggah; walk away while you can.

I was like, "DAAAAAMNNNNN!"
My man!
That's what's up.
Man look at you,
You got that street lingo locked,
With your 9MM Glock, no doubt it's cocked.
Looking like you're fresh off the cell block
Covered in dreadlocks.
In your little drop-top
You probably just copped from a chop shop,
Moving mad weight out the back of the barbershop.
Son, you're convincing on so many levels,
But I see your ignorant black ass
And I raise you two white devils.
You wanna talk gangsta?
I'm 'bout to give you a quick history lesson.

In 1850 marijuana was added to
The United States pharmacopeia.
In regards to marijuana, there was no phobia, Just utopia,
For white America, it was like life on the Ponderosa.
From Saratoga to North Dakota,
Minnesota to Oklahoma,
Folks were having apple pie and Coca-Cola.
Feeling sober,
Like they had their own personal Oprah
Saying, 'Today you get a Toyota Corolla.'

And marijuana was being prescribed
For a variety of ailments from
Dysentery to mental disorders,
Excessive menstrual bleeding in mothers and daughters
No doubt a tall order, competitive prices got slaughtered.
And based on the positive results that
Americans were seeing,
They started believing that indeed they would be needing
Marijuana as a legitimate source of healing.
And oh what a feeling when the dealers came dealing,
And truth be told, to the young and old,
All across America, patented marijuana
Tinctures were being sold.

Forward to 1930 and Harry J. Anslinger
Was appointed Commissioner of the
Federal Bureau of Narcotics,
Sort of like a 1930's version of the DEA.
Yet white folks were still selling marijuana,
And white folks were still getting paid.
Now Anslinger's good friend was
William Randolph Hearst
And Big Willy Hearst owned some
Of the largest newspapers in America
Like the New York Journal and
The San Francisco Examiner.
If the printing business was the mafia, then
Hearst was the Don
And he figured that he could make a lot more paper,
If he had a monopoly on the paper
That his competitors' newspapers were printed on.
So all across the globe, Hearst bought
Rain forests by the acres,
To ensure that he was the sole crusader, the
Chief manipulator
Who would monopolized the production and
Shipment of paper.
He decided that within a few short years when
It came to paper,
He would be, 'The Man.'

And I guess Mother Nature didn't like
The idea of the desecration of her land,
Because she conspired with Life, and goddamn,
If they didn't throw a monkey wrench
In that motherfucker's plans.

Because right about that time a machine was invented,
Called the decorticator,
And it had the ability on a massive scale
To turn hemp into paper.
Which would seriously threaten
William Randolph Hearst's dough,
And rightfully so, because on the low, with just one blow
That technology could single-handedly
Constipate his cash flow.
Hemp could be harvested every six months,
Trees, as you know, took about 20 years to grow.

But Hearst was one tough nut to crack,
And being a fat cat, he did the math and
Was like, 'Fuck that!'
He figured that he didn't even need the strap
In order to make the entire industry tap.
He decided to clap back with a preemptive attack
That would be far more exact than the
Typical rat-a-tat-tat.

Bought him a bureaucrat to squash that yikkity-yak
And make sure all them whippersnaps fall back.
And if you're thinking,
'Can he actually do that?'
Come on son, being a white male in America?
Stop that, you know he got that.

William Randolph Hearst went to
See his boy H.J. Anslinger
At the Federal Narcotics Bureau.
Anslinger was like, 'Randy! Long time no see baby.'
Hearst replied, 'Harry, for the intrusion pardon me,
But I've got a matter that requires your sense of urgency
You see I've got enemies with technologies,
And they're threatening me.'
'Word?'
'Well...theoretically.'

'I need you to turn this herbal remedy
Into a felony with severe penalties.
No pleasantries, no empathy, no clemency.
Straight intensity, treat it like leprosy.
Kill that shit quick, like the brevity of a Kennedy's fidelity.
I've got billions spent.
I need you to outlaw this hemp.
Because if anyone thinks I'm going to lose my investment,

No such luck,
Nothing can stop me Harry, I'm all the way up.'

Of course, I'm paraphrasing,
But after contemplating, I didn't find it too amazing
That Anslinger was definitely down for the cause.
But how could he pull it off
When so many Americans were
Profiting from hemp within the laws?
And regardless of how committed
Anslinger was to ride or die,
To find a sucker and justify why said
Sucker needed to be crucified.
There was no way Americans were gonna
Comply and allow themselves to be Shanghaied,
Unless of course, they were terrified.
Now listen hun, one lesson that I always teach my son,
Is when you have fear, you don't need a gun,
Because fear gets shit done.

Anyway, to get the Senate's dedication
To sign the legislation against the medication
Anslinger was just the ideal guy
To formulate and deliver a bold-faced lie.
One that would horrify and later become
The battle cry of every red-blooded American.

Make them scream it from the bottom of their lungs
To the top of their throats.
Act 1, Scene 2: Enter the Negro,
America's favorite scapegoat.

Anslinger later testified in front of the Senate and I quote,
"There are over 100,000 marijuana smokers
In the United States,
Most of which are negroes.
Their satanic jazz music is a result of marijuana use.
Reefer makes darkies think they're as good as white men,
Furthermore, marijuana causes white women
To seek sexual relations with negroes."

Needless to say, marijuana became illegal that same day.
Or sometime shortly thereafter.
But what cannot be denied,
No matter how hard you try
Is that Anslinger was a racist gun for hire.
These two devils did conspire,
Not a single shot fired.
Billions were made from this little paper trade,
No one got tripped up by Jake,
Because as usual, when it comes to America
Conspiring against Blacks,
Law enforcement was in on the take.

Hearst made mad cake from this crusade,
His wealth and namesake still on parade.
And if this little narrative has left you shook,
Then all you've got to do is look,
And you'll see that in the past 100 years,
America has changed neither the play nor the playbook.
Pay attention whenever Main Stream Media rants,
And you'll see that they've added a few more scapegoats,
Like Muslims, Mexicans, and immigrants.

Now back to my little gangster rappers in search of glory
With your little cockamamie stories.
Your inflammatory allegories about your inventory.
Your guts, your glory, your guns, your story,
They bore me.
This here is self-explanatory,
Hearst's caper was all about paper,
Yet you don't even own the copyrighted paper
That your bullshit lyrics are printed on.
But you want to convince me of how
Gangster you are in your little sing-alongs.

So here I am, once again
Transforming boys to men.
The lesson that I intend
Is to show you the futility of your Mac 10.

To have you comprehend
That your end will most likely be ten in the Penn,
With a not so gentleman friend who attends
To your rear end every now and then
Like Adebisi listening to Eminem.
While splitting you like dividends,
Spreading you like an OB-GYN,
Rev-ing you like RPM.
Have you screaming like you're at the MGM,
With your little lady friend and y'all
Just hit the jackpot for the Big Ten.
You've never been to London
But now you're having nightmares about Big Ben,
You might get some sleep, but it ain't R.E.M
Meditate all you want, but you can't find Zen.
For protection, you could become a
Muslim and try not to offend,
But then again, you could just follow the
Trend and be born again,
And start believing in the three wise men.
Start praying to that white man from Bethlehem
Who was 33 with no girlfriend,
But always seen with 12 other men,
Like he was coaching a team on ESPN,
But that's a whole 'nother poem.

The point is my friend
You can never transcend your bitter end,
Until you understand the difference
Between you and them.
You see, real gangsters don't carry guns,
They carry pens.

9-2-5

He got up early this morning,
Hugged his child and kissed his wife,
There are bills to be paid,
So he's off to his nine to five.
His goals aren't written,
To please his boss is his major scheme,
Trading his time for money chasing
That elusive American dream.

He hates the job but has no one
In whom he can confide.
That whenever he punches that time clock,
He's committing spiritual suicide.
Dying inside, crying inside.
Looking at his boss, murmuring,
"God, I wish somebody would just shoot ya."
Not knowing that he's the god
Who is molding this cancerous future.

He doesn't want to think about it,
But his fate is sealed,

He's thirty-five with a thirty-year mortgage,
And he thought it was a steal.
For real.
If he gets laid off, my God, how will he manage?
He's got a child in kindergarten,
One on the way and nothing saved for college.
Gotta keep up with the Jones'
So he upgrades his car,
His wife objects to the move
And it leaves emotional scars.

To be truthful,
She no longer makes love to him like she used to.
Those moans no longer seem homegrown,
As she disconnects the caller ID,
Went out and got her a cellular phone.
But he has no time to focus on that,
Gotta hustle the insurance and car loan,
He grabs his briefcase,
Kissed her on the cheekbone
Left his backbone at home
Before he hurries to the war zone.

"Heya Bob."
Fronting like he's fulfilled in that bullshit job.
The boss threatens his security,

Demanding more production for his time
"Yes sir, very well sir, but of course sir."
Frustrated and emotionally castrated,
He comes home and treats his wife like a swine.
He now works longer hours,
Depressed and emotionally insecure
So now in bed, he's a sexual bore.
But he keeps pressing on,
Because at sixty-five
He wishes to be socially secured.

Living paycheck to paycheck,
Financially, he's one big mess.
He tried to refinance his home
Just to find that for the past five years,
He's been paying only interest.
No doubt, he's stressed,
Low on dough and just
Got taxed by his HMO.
You don't know?
Realizing that nine to five ain't no joke,
And J-O-B, be an acronym for,
'Journey of the Broke.'
He watches his dreams go up in smoke,
Like a practical joke,
But gotta keep that mask on for the town folks.

Steady steppin' and fetchin'
Skinning and grinning,
Posing and posturing,
Shucking and jiving
Poor clown barely surviving.
He's been working so hard,
And nothing, nothing has he gained,
He grabs a bottle of Scotch,
Trying to drown the pain.
Now he constantly fights with his wife,
And to him, she's no longer nice.
And he has this gut feeling
That the postman has been ringing twice.

Screaming, "Dear God,
Why did you curse me?"
But as a man thinketh, so is he.
Not knowing that he's the god
That created this painful destiny
And this ugly reality.
He's not schooled in the
Powers of the subconscious.
Not knowing that
The unseen controls the scene,
He died the minute that he lacked

The courage to pursue his dreams.

You can never kill
That quiet whispering voice inside of you,
It will haunt you, taunt you
Pick out a wreath and casket for you.
He's a sheep, schooled in the art of following,
Now his soul's hollering.
He's got high blood pressure and an ulcer,
He's a victim to this slave culture
Not knowing that's how life damages ya,
When you refuse to live your dream.
Pursue your passion because
Faith is the evidence of things not seen,
I encourage you; step out on your dreams.
Now watch as life shatters
This poor soul in the next scene.

He came home early, and emotionally he was hot,
Found the mailman delivering to his wife's G spot,
Representing all the flavors of Hip Hop.
Have her heaving like she needed a cough drop
He didn't even know that she was flexible like that.
The mailman was sucking chocolate syrup
Off the finger that held her wedding ring,
Poor soul didn't even know that his wife

Owned a leopard skin G string.

The mailman turned his wife into a play station.
Working her like she was chained on a plantation,
Dropping strokes like he was chief of the Zulu nation
Like he was the good deacon, and she needed saving.
Like he was Jesus delivering salvation.
Like she was the rainforest
And he was planting vegetation,
Convulsing like a fiend
Who had not taken his medication.
And in her eyes, you could see her appreciation.
She looked like a slave
Who had just heard the emancipation proclamation,
And to Massa, she was showing her utmost gratification.

She had the candles and the hot wax,
The mailman was still in his tube socks.
Had his wife legs pinned behind her neck,
Bouncing her like one of his rubber checks.
He watched as the strong young buck,
Unhooked his wife like a tow truck,
Grabbed the back of her hair and instructs,
"Come on baby, blow on it for luck."

In divorce court, homeboy had a fit,

Alimony, child support, he lost half his shit.
The new car that he bought,
The mailman was whipping it.
His Scotch, the mailman sipping it,
His wife, no doubt, hitting it.
So later that night from the roof of his office
He took his life,
Because he discovered,
He could not capture the American dream.
Working nine to five.

Predator

I observed you from afar,
Even though I knew you were taken.
I heard your man throws a good dick,
And brings home the bacon.
But when I looked deeply,
I could see some emptiness in your eyes,
That's when I knew I could step up
And get my slice of the pie.

I knew in some particular area,
Your man had to be slippin'
Now, if only I could find out where,
I could exploit it and make you start trippin'.
I knew my game had to be tight, my shit...legit.
'Else you could just hit me with that,
"See you in the next lifetime." bullshit.
So naw, I stepped back and methodically planned my shit,
You're about to become the victim of a
Cold, calculated hit.

I proceeded to introduce myself,

And explained how lucky your man must be
To have here on Earth, a girl of your heavenly beauty.
You smiled and looked away, well in fact, you blushed.
That's when I knew I was making progress,
But chill playboy, no need to rush.

I said, "Good-bye." and walked away confident
That the foundation was laid,
Knowing that it was only a matter of time
Before I would be getting paid.
The next day I saw you waiting for the bus,
And though I kept my composure,
I was overcome by lust.
I told you I was going in your direction,
And offered to give you a ride.
You got in,
Now I'm one step closer
To moving your man to the side.

We conversed a bit,
And I found in what area this brother had failed,
Though he may take care of business
He doesn't pay attention to details.
He never seems to notice when you get your hair,
Your nails, your face done.
His mind is focused on business,

And he seldom has time for fun.
Though you're an angel,
For you, he never made a fuss,
So I stepped up to the plate and told you,
"Baby, please, you're gorgeous!"

Starving for attention,
Of course, you gave up the digits,
Now it was only a matter of time
To my will, you would submit.
You gave up the number,
Saying we could only be friends,
Lovers; NEVER!
I thought, "How naive,
Yeah, baby, yeah friends, whatever."

I said, "Sweetheart please, as gorgeous as you are,
I am honored just to know your name."
Hence, the beginning of the game.
Whenever you needed to talk,
I was there to hold your hand as we walked.
Whenever you needed to cry,
I was there to dry your eyes.
Whenever you were down,
I built you a crown.
Whenever we were together

I made sure the time spent was a blast.
I made you close your eyes
And put away all the horrors of the past.
I promised to take your troubles away,
As I placed a pedestal under your feet
But the fact of the matter is,
I'm just a dealer of deceit.

Soon she came to see me
As one of the nicest men, she's ever met.
And sure enough, I saw her as just some chick
I ain't fucked yet.
Yeah, I knew she was caught in my emotional net,
But still, she needed a few more lies to get her wet.

So I compliment her on the clothes she would wear.
Paid attention whenever she did her hair,
Asked her about her day and her bullshit career
Promised her silk and fine cashmere,
As I whispered sweet nothings in her ear.
I told her how she made my heart flutter
Whenever she drew near,
And to be without her is what I feared,
And no matter what happens, I will always be there.
And, "God, if...if only you knew how much I cared."
And I told her a bunch of other bullshit

That women love to hear.

Needless to say, she saw me as a friend,
And her man the foe.
Took me in bed not knowing
She's being manipulated,
By a deceitful Scorpio.

And I remembered when she said,
She wasn't with my plan.
She had a man,
Even showed me the engagement band,
But still,
She fell for my program,
Of candle lights and slow jams
Now I'm reaching for the Trojans,
And she ain't even thinking about her man.

Your man just left, and he's barely out the door,
Now you're calling,
Telling me that I made you cum
Like you never came before.
Not realizing that a simple test of life,
You've just failed,
Now you're reaching for me,
Thinking that you've exhaled.

You don't want me to leave,
And you're begging me to stay,
But I'm a Predator baby,
And you weak girls straight up, my prey.

You had a good man,
Yes, he wasn't perfect,
Now here comes the Predator
To exploit your weakness.
Whenever you have a good man,
Never focus on the small details he's lacking,
'Cause there's a Predator out there, somewhere, watching.
So even though you beg, we can't be together.
Honey, I thought you knew,
Besides, you cheated on your man,
Who's to say you won't cheat on me too?

I need a woman I can work with,
Not a superficial girl from around the way,
Who is gonna jump from bed to bed
Because of a compliment that I forgot to pay.
So when you come with your soap opera story,
Wanting to be my bride,
All I gotta say is,
"Sorry hun, but thanks for the ride."

Copout

Forget the sellout,
Tonight it's the copout,
That I want to talk about.
The ignorant negro that's
Quick to come out his mouth,
Yell and shout,
Puff and pout,
'Bout his financial drought.
Telling me that the white man
Keeps watching his whereabouts.
The same negro that has six kids down south,
And has yet to put bread in their mouths.

I'm sick of negroes using their blackness as a crutch,
Telling me the "White man" done did them such and such.
Saying that the Jews are robbing us blind,
And in our neighborhoods
Korean stores are all they find.
Complaining that the Arabs
Are pimping us like whores,
Yet he just dropped half his check,

In that Arab liquor store.
Saying we should make it
So these damn Chinese restaurants starve,
Five minutes later, he's coming back
With four wings, fried hard.

I am not trying to hear about your conspiracy,
Not when you're high off that Hennessy.
Coming back from your spending spree
In your chromed out Cherokee,
With your ruff neck company
Bragging about your felony.
Steady telling me
About your calamity,
And how the 'White man,'
Is the cause of your every agony.

I am sick and tired,
Of negroes living a life
That's gonna cause them to self-destruct,
Then copout by using their blackness as a crutch.
A lot of these negroes,
I'm not feeling them so much.

Copouts, quick to complain about
The racist laws that politicians wrote,

They complain all night,
But election day, they won't even vote.
"The white man won't give me no job."
First words out their mouths,
Going on interviews, all ebonics the fuck out.
I know cats late for work every single day jack,
And when they get fired,
"Man, that shit would've never happened
If I wasn't black."

Ignorant negroes quick to run to the mall,
And every dime they earned, spent,
Knowing damn well they're two months
Behind on their rent.
Trying to justify it with that ignorant chat,
But can't explain to me exactly
How the white man made you do that?

Tell me how he makes you spend
All your money at Christmas time,
So that until you get that tax refund
You don't have a dime.
Ignorant negroes quick to spit that,
"Yeah, man, it's all good."
But when life goes wrong,
They riot and tear up

Their own damn neighborhoods.

I am not saying that racism doesn't exist,
But my skin ain't no crutch,
When life goes wrong, I'm going to stand up.
I am not about to come out of my mouth,
Yell and shout, puff and pout
Because the negro that does that
Knows not what he speaks about.

Look at my history,
Am I not the epitome of success?
I caused pyramids to manifest
And left devils impressed.
Survived the stress,
When my child, they molest,
But nevertheless,
Taught their kids how to love and caress.
Nurtured their suckling on my delicate breasts.

I toppled Mt. Everest and rode their pony express.
Slaughtered monsters in the Loch Ness
So they could go West,
It was on my back that they built UPS.
Check the DNA of this country's success,
And you'll find my blood embedded in her progress.

Before my arrival, this country was a mess.
If it wasn't for my free labor,
There would be no Gettysburg address.

But that's one truth they will never profess on CBS,
Tune in to the news at ten
When you're ready for the real BS.
I stood on the front-line
Of their battlefields when they were in distress,
My neck was a rung on their ladder of success.
They raped my princess, and made her a mistress,
YES!
It was on my back that America built her success.
So when you talk endurance,
I AM THAT LITMUS TEST.
Forget what you've heard
I'm here to testify inasmuch,
THAT THIS BLACK SKIN
AIN'T NEVER BEEN NO CRUTCH!

Too Big To Hate

If you came to have the Christian experience,
Go get baptized and celebrate what you did.
And if you came to be a convict,
Then by all means, do your bid.
And if you came to have the Muslim experience,
Then As-Salam-u-Alaykum kid.
And if being anything other than
Black leaves you pissed
Then I salute you with the black fist.
In other words, I will never dis'.
You see, I don't give a good goddamn
If you're an argumentative liberal representative
Or one of these talkative Christian conservatives,
Who's so full of shit, they need a laxative,
In order to allow me to live my prerogative.

Casing my life, like they're a cop with the K-9 Rover
But if their dirt ever came to light,
It would be game over.
They would be up in the pulpit singing
That, 'Somebody done me wrong' song.

Ain't that right Eddie Long?

You see, it doesn't matter to me
If you're atheist or agnostic.
Faithful husband, or
You've got a thousand side chicks,
Pimp in the streets, or pimp in the pulpit.
I don't care if you're straighter than the poles
That my favorite dancers embrace at night,
Or if you've found a way
To channel your inner Rainbow Bright.
Doesn't matter to me if you're uptight about Pro-Life
Or you're a black transvestite on a hunger strike,
Waving strobe lights in broad daylight,
Trying to bring attention to gay rights
By saying that you hate whites.

I am not troubled by the dark,
Because I AM The Light.
So in spite of the night, I find delight
In the fact that shit ain't always bright.
And I don't need you to be wrong
So that my little ego can validate
That once again, I'm right.

So make no apologies honey,

Go ahead and be yourself
Because if it wasn't for the contrast,
I probably wouldn't know myself.
And whatever you came here to be,
I don't need to agree,
In order to support you fully.
The world is your blackboard
And your intention is your chalk,
And whenever you meet people
Who are spiritually aware,
You never have to explain your walk.

So with me, you don't have to sit on the fence
A difference of opinion doesn't
Have to lead to indifference.
Whatever you came here to do,
That is your rendition.
So you will never hear a petition,
Or a poem, from me convincing
You of what road will lead you home,
What race or gender needs to be in your bed
In order to make you moan, groan.

No, that is not my calling, not my work.
Because when you were created
No one said, "Now that you're here on Earth,

Your purpose is to please Kirk."
Please conform to his ideologies
Fuck your free will, adopt his philosophies.
Disregard what your heart
Is telling you every single day
Because Kirk Nugent's way is the ONLY way.
Such an idea would be offensive to the soul,
It would immediately provoke your wrath
So what I'm saying to you is,
"I'm staying out of your business
Because I understand your path, is your path."

Now, with that said,
Don't come over here trying to convince me
Of the correctness of your philosophy,
You came here to be you, not to recruit me.
And I see beauty in diversity.
So I'm not trying to hear your lecture and conjecture
Of how it ought to be in this sector.
Don't bring me the nectar from your exposed
Breast of bullshit and ask me to nurse it.
Because I'll straight up curse it,
Spit on it like it's the worst shit.
Rip you apart in a poem like you deserved it,
The name is Kirk Nugent and nobody
Tells me who the fuck to worship.

My mind is too strong to be trapped in a prison
I cannot be enslaved with isms and schisms.
I AM a spiritual giant;
Not an emotional child locked in some bullshit system.
I observe the herd, but I don't go with them,
I understand Universal Laws,
So you ain't looking at no victim.
Your limiting ideas are like spam mail
And I just don't click them.
So you could never get me to hate someone
Based on society's decisions
Or their predispositions, their race, their nationality,
Their gender, their sexual orientation, their religion.
That none sense is so far off my chart
So don't even start.
You wanna do something?
Show me the content of your heart.
What is the meaning of your actions?
Is love a part of your fashion,
And do you move with compassion?

So my actions can never make me a liar,
Because I came to embrace the ENTIRE
Human experience,
And I know for some folks,

That just doesn't make any sense
As they observe,
Kirk, where is your racial pride?
Aren't you supposed to be a proud black man?
While others say,
"Sounds like you're siding with the enemy
You don't sound like a patriotic American."
But patriotism is the religion of the terrified
And I did not come to compartmentalize
Nor did I come to embrace the narrative of fiction,
So yes, how dare I choose to live my life
On the outskirts of your definitions?

Now you have these so-called evangelicals,
Who would never publicly nor privately,
Admit that my life matter,
But every chance they get,
They want to flood me with their bullshit chatter.
With conviction, trying to convince me of what to believe,
'So Kirk, this is the way the story goes,
There's a special place for those who love the Lord
And there's a special place for his foes.'
But understand me when I say
That the only things you will ever believe
Are the things that you don't know.
So basically what you're saying to me is,

'Kirk, here's a bunch of shit that I don't know,
And based on that, I want you to follow me.'
But sorry son, this ain't Oz
And my name ain't Dorothy.

To ask me to pray to the God of the ones
Who lynched my ancestors when they took flight
The ones who came burning crosses during the night
Tuskegee Project my DNA like they owned the copyright,
Told white lies and Emmitt Till my life,
Deny my civil rights, and murder
Unarmed black boys at traffic lights.
Without me asking you, 'Yo, da fuck I look like?'
Is to ask me to push the agenda of white supremacy,
And that just doesn't make sense to me.

Now in your arrogance,
You might claim that I'm disrespecting your scripture
But my question is, 'When was the last time
You asked a Jew
To bow down to the God of Hitler?'
So while others might ingest
Some nonsensical dogma without blinking
Oh, please believe, I fucks with critical thinking.

Besides, such a narrow perspective of ALL THAT IS

Needs to die with the generation gap,
As a matter of fact, ain't nobody got time for that.
And because I'm black,
Doesn't necessarily make me a Democrat,
Stop that!
At the same time,
A constipated elephant doesn't appeal to me,
So you're going to have a very hard time defining me.
It should start becoming painfully obvious
That based on the definitions that you're trying to bring
The box that you're putting me in,
I'm simply not living in.
I AM philosophically promiscuous,
Go find the synonym.

And right now, we might not be the majority,
But they're many like me
And we don't care how much you hate us,
Your ignorance doesn't scare us,
No, not in the Age of Aquarius.
We know that the Universe
Will no longer tolerate your crap,
Do you want food for thought?
Well, we've got plenty of that.
Pull up a chair, and we'll pour you a cup,
Do you want to be enlightened?

Well, go ahead and lighten the fuck up.

So you see, you can go ahead and pardon me,
Because I don't care
About someone else's sexuality, B
In the Land of the free, I leave that to the GOP,
He's gay; I'm straight, more for me.
So logically I live in harmony
The pure simplicity of letting others be.
Now folks see the peace that I have within
So they come searching like
I'm some sort of guru for them.
And they say, "Oh Radiant One of the Poetic Realm,
Please tell us how it's done."
And I say, "It's simple,
Just mind your fucking business son."

I No Longer Write About Depression

First I was afraid, no doubt, petrified.
Reflecting on my life
Wondering how I survived.
I recall my childhood,
Always wanting to run away or commit suicide.
Always fearing having company,
Because that's when I would be stripped of my pride.
Esteem tossed to the side
As parents transformed into Jekyll and Hyde.
I recall being the best and the brightest in school
Winning a full scholarship, awards, mad stuff,
Only to come home and feel like you're not good enough.

I remember kneeling by my bed praying to God
For the end of my days.
Walking by the cemetery
Envying the lucky bastard in the grave.
I remember wanting out so badly,
That I wouldn't take my medicine for Sickle Cells,
Hoping I would have a crisis and it would just kill me.
I remember being unclothed and disrobed

And stripped down to my little white
Fruit of The Loom brief
And being beaten until the blood broke
Freely from my skin,
And as a child, trouble was something I was never in.
My dad justified it by saying, responsibility
He was teaching.

He used all manner of electrical wires,
To ensure that my eight-year-old skin stayed on fire.
By nine I concluded that parent's love
Was just too much for any child to desire.
And if you looked into my eyes, it was obvious,
They had successfully extinguished my fire.

But given a choice, if I had to choose
I would choose the beatings over the emotional abuse.
Even though I can recall being beaten
Until my spirit laughed no more,
Cried no more, loved no more.
Self-worth packed up and walked,
Teachers would send for my parents, asking,
"What's wrong with Kirk?
He's so bright, but he doesn't talk."

Would you?

After being beaten damn near half to death
Because you forgot to feed the dogs.
To this day I can hear both parents' voices reminding me
Of how much they regretted bringing me into this world,
And back then I nurtured suicidal thoughts like
Steinbeck nurtured The Pearl.

Sickle Cells had me laying in hospital beds
Pondering what's taking God so long to kill me.
My parents were good Christians,
My God, they deserved to be happy.
I was sick of being stripped of my self-worth,
Robbed of my esteem,
Feeling like an expense waiting to be disposed of,
Always feeling unworthy of.
I felt no more needed than a pair of metal glove,
And I tried to mask the pain
By acting like I wasn't fiending for their love.
But who was I fooling?
I wanted it more than O.J wanted an alibi,
And in the process of trying to gain their acceptance
I inadvertently committed spiritual suicide.
.

But parents don't care,
They found new and improved ways
To batter and bruise me,

Humiliate and refuse me.
Mom did the church thing on Sundays,
Dad read the Bible damn near daily,
And I hated dogs and Christianity.

I lived in a world of illusions and hypocrisy.
By the time I discovered this poetry
Depression was in bed with me,
Loneliness slept next to me,
Unworthiness got dressed with me.
The pen and paper fought to maintain my sanity
For my spirit had long abandoned me.

Low esteem was nothing new,
And eye contact was just something I didn't do.
God forbid I had to talk to you
I kept my eyes focused on my shoe.
Plastic smiles conveniently constructed
To mask internal rain,
And all I wrote about was depression and pain.

I was walking that thin line
Between being suicidal and homicidal.
I had a .45 and a Gloc nine,
And knew if someone pushed me
We would both lose our minds.

Because back then I wasn't trying to give a fuck,
I was young, black, armed, and dangerous.
Thinking to leave this world in gunsmoke
Would be glorious.
Back then, me and my Jamaican clique
Were re-defining the term notorious,
We were ready to die
And these gang recruiters were adoring us.
But even the toughest gang member
Knew we were crazy Jamaicans
And they best not be provoking us.

Before you could say the words "Racial profile."
I matured to that level
Where one starts becoming aware of racism.
Now my anger, frustration, and hatred grew to
Another level,
Convinced that this white God was against me,
I was determined to team up with the devil.
I would watch nightly news reports
Of police brutality and it fueled my rage,
Wasn't long before me and the devil were on
The same page.

I mean totally in sync

And my only goal before I die
Was to murder an entire precinct.
I went against the grain, fought against the norm,
Masturbated to thoughts of putting
Holes in these blue uniforms.
I was tired of watching the oppressors
Wrapping nooses around the necks of the oppressed.
Tired being the victim, tired of being the oppressed,
Tired of being helpless.
I wasn't looking for that Dr. King
"We shall overcome" type justice,
Naw, I was pissed,
My guns were livid, and the devil was like,
"Kirk, we can do this!"

But God;
But God has a funny way of molding the future
Found out I was soon to be a father,
Decided that this lifestyle could go no further.
I remember being in the delivery room,
Looking into my son's eyes
Thinking I don't care what the psychologist,
The psychiatrist, the psychoanalyst writes,
This cycle of abuse dies tonight.

I vowed to him, "I will never shed your blood,

Nor intentionally bring a tear to your eye.
And you will know that you are loved
From the day you are born until the day you die."
Gave him my name, which was a selfish thing to do
But for once in my life
I wanted to hear a parent say the words,
"Kirk, I love you."

So, who knew that it would take a baby to change my life?
Who knew that it would take a child
To change the way that I write?
Because I no longer write about depression,
Through my child, I've found myself.
I no longer write about depression
Because Kirk doesn't get depressed.
This world can't make me stress,
Perturbed, perplexed,
Anguished, or distressed.
With the obstacles of this world
I'm neither moved nor impressed.

My God has found
And delivered me from all my fears.
Into a well of hope,
He's transformed those years of tears.
Yes, He was there,

When no one called, no one came, no one cared.

And if I had to do it all over again,
If He placed me in the fire, put my head to the gun,
I wouldn't change a single thing,
Because I love the person I've become.
I no longer write about depression,
My spirit can never be eaten by flesh,
The People's Poet is not the devil's conquest.
I've got a story to tell and through it
I've resurrected many souls from the dead,
So if spiritually you're empty,
Then tell the world I've got bread.
I no longer write about depression!

Instead, I let my soul manifest,
Flew the cuckoo's nest
Took the litmus test,
I'm here to testify, so can I get a witness?
I've placed fear and doubt under cardiac arrest.
Pulled faith, hope, and confidence from my war chest,
Laid all insecurities to rest.
My spirit has returned
And vowed never again to be oppressed.

I no longer write about depression;

Instead, I've strapped on persistence as my life vest,
Now I'm heading north by north-west
And I dare depression to run come test.
I've dropped the burden I've been carrying
Around for years,
Lift my eyes unto the hills and declared,
"Regardless of what negativity parents had to share,
I AM WORTHY OF BEING HERE!"

My son has taught me how to love and how to live,
Through grace, I've risen,
And I have nothing but love to give.
My past is buried in the past
And from this day forth, I shall live.
I no longer write about depression
Because by God, I've learned how to forgive.

She Was Everything To Me

It was on the eve of a previous life that we first met,
She foretold my trials and tribulations,
Promised that she would return
To walk me through a thousand deaths.
She said that I had to heal myself
Before I could heal the nation.
Told me it was eons ago
When she first walked
From the ocean floors
Holding Time in her hands.

She said that she sat
In the corner of a distant galaxy
Observing the vanity of man.
She traded the Gods,
Two pulsars, a nebula, and a supernova,
So they would advance her to the future
Just to warn me of my impending disaster.
She said, "Here take this, it will help you think clearer."

Now here we are present day,

And the pieces are finally coming together.
I searched her eyes wondering
Why it took me forever to embrace her.
To invest in her my emotional currency
How could I have overlooked her beauty?
I must have been deaf,
Because I swore
Her eyes said that they loved me.

The scent of her body shackled my heart,
And arrested my soul.
She declared that my story must be told.
Yes, she was pushy, raw, uncut,
Spoke from the gut.
If her heart felt it,
Then that was the lesson her tongue dished,
Women despised her, and men labeled her a bitch.
One lesson she taught me way before I was twelve
Is that bitch was just an acronym
For Babe in Total Control of Herself.

At fifteen, when I was bent on destroying the world,
Rebelling against what parents had taught me.
Realizing that Christianity
Was synonymous with hypocrisy.
This so-called democracy was fuckery,

And Babylon live fi murda we.

The only public housing we build are penitentiaries.
I live in a system that lives to divide and conquer,
Saying, "This doesn't concern you; it's about gay rights."
Or it's about women's rights,
Or civil rights or the rights of the handicap
Knowing damn well, it's about human rights.
So their plight is my plight,
And their fight, my fight.

I've met hypocrites claiming
That they serve a living God,
Damn near sixty-five,
And they still haven't lived.
Saying they worship a loving God,
But have no love to give.
A God of peace, a God of mercy,
A forgiving God, a God of truth.
These same hypocrites hate fags,
Niggers, spics, kikes, chinks, gooks.
They've never shown mercy
To that homeless mother in the hood,
And they've yet to forgive their parents
For their ungodly childhood.
It came to a point where I could no longer

Tell the difference between volunteer and victim,
And I just wanted to take a dull knife
And gut this bullshit system.

It was that night; she came to me,
Told me to close both my eyes in order to see.
She declared, "Boy, shut your mouth and speak."
There were more mysteries in her eyes
Than the Bible and Koran combined.
She told me that I was a vessel,
But I was given limited time.
She told me that, 'The Unpopular Truth.'
Will be difficult for many to take,
Therefore I will judge you
By the enemies that you make.
Now close your eyes and walk by faith.
Now Kirk, tell me why do fools
Always find other fools to emulate?
Why does hate so easily contaminate?
Tell me what makes the great, great?
And what causes gods to believe
They're nothing more than mere primates?

I said, "Well, I see beautiful women
Trying to hide insecurities
Plastering on makeup all day.

But like all other false foundation,
It just washes away.
I see women failing to realize
That until you sleep with a man
All you've met is his representative.
An ambassador for his penis,
The diplomat who for the candlelight dinners
He's willing to splurge,
Sleep with him once
And the real dictator will emerge."

I speak for the forgotten soldier
Who bled to death in some cold,
Dark, damp, disgusting trench.
Died for his convictions regarding democracy,
Just to be buried in hypocrisy.
The same government that
He died for sold drugs to his family.
Reinvest the profits and built his son
A lifetime stay in a modern penitentiary.
Oh, I cry for the pawns in this game of chess.

Wanting to make a difference,
But they shut down our spirituality,
Brainwashed the entire faculty.
I see unseen hands pitting you against me

And me against you,
In boardrooms, they collectively divide the two.
Telling you that my black skull you should bash,
Telling me, you're nothing but white trash.

We're both pawns in this New World Order,
Because even in your white skin
You're not allowed to cross their Elitist border.
I see the devil's signature all over their dollar,
I see nations being deceived by Rhode scholars.
I see sheep walking down a path
That they have yet to investigate,
World Power being dictated by initiates.
Population control is the goal
As devils barter for your soul.
Slowly changing morality,
Programming you towards homosexuality.
Can't you see, they're tightening the noose?
Don't you get it?
Two men can never reproduce.

But the puppeteers have you in a trance,
Have you killing your babies,
Before returning to the dance.
Fine you with a slap on the wrist
So it's not even a deterrent,

Yes, I see disaster brewing in the undercurrents.

They reap the benefits while to
Some distant God you pray,
Notice how they change your Sabbath to SUN-day.
She said, "Kirk, you're preaching again,
History has burnt many preachers at the stake."
My response was, "I speak the Unpopular Truth,
So judge me by the enemies that I make."
The truth that I speak, until the day I die,
Them words I will defend,
If a man refuses to live in peace,
He should rest in it then.

I see poets trying to copy my style,
Not knowing that I drop my lines,
In encrypted rhymes,
Too subtle for the average mind.
So they run out and kill their dreams,
While I execute mine.

I looked in her eyes and the world became right,
Tasted her tongue, and History stood corrected.
There was something in her kiss
That consumed me immediately,
She held court with my heart

And I wanted no mercy.
Her body, a tulip covered with midnight dew,
She inspired everything that I had ever hoped to do.
I buried myself in her love
And was resurrected a better man,
The thing that she gave me to think more clearly,
I held in my left hand.

Her flames engulfed my soul,
She poured fire in my eyes
As she prepared me for this role.
I was drenched in her love,
Soaked in her sweetness,
Doused with desire.
I became pregnant with passion,
And gave birth to inspired action.
She was dinner by candlelight,
Sex by moonlight,
A spiritual delight,
The first date that ever stayed overnight.
She's the reason why I stand
Before you, here tonight.
To true love, she led the way,
The reason these eyes have never strayed.
The one who restored my sanity,
In short, this woman was my Poetry.

And On the 8th Day

You can easily tell the inspiration behind someone's work by merely observing the results of said work. Take the black woman for instance. It's evident that when God created her, He didn't only work through lunch, but he hung a 'Do not disturb' sign on the door. Just observing her features, both physically and spiritually, it is obvious that when God created her, He was having the time of His life because she's a reflection of uncompromising good taste.

Think about it; He has already created the planets and the poles, the galaxies and black holes, thunder and tornadoes, earthquakes and floods, hurricanes, the Milky Way, infinite dimensions with different densities, dragons and unicorns, goblins and giants, dinosaurs and DNA, and then He said, 'How the fuck can I top this?'

If you observe the black woman, you know goddamn well she was not created with no, 'Let there be...' type of commandment. Oh, hell no, not with the kind of attention to details that went into her. So to prepare Himself for the ultimate task at hand, He first created Jamaica so that He could harvest the most excellent weed on the planet so that He, the Lord thy God, could have the correct meditation and inspiration before getting started.

He then called a board meeting for a brainstorming session, which lasted 777 billion trillion years, after which it was decided that God would create a Light Being that would absorb Light and therefore appears to be dark. No one in Heaven thought that shit was possible. Lucifer got cast out for running off at the mouth and doubting the magic of what would be known as the black woman. Every other Being was created in an instant, but God had the black woman marinating in melanin for two thousand and twenty-two years, then He soaked her in the sunshine for another hundred and forty-four thousand years. He decided that this Being would be so exceptional, so magical... think about it, every other Being on Earth hair would buckle under the weight of gravity; however, the black woman's hair would defy gravity, it would naturally reach towards the heavens so that God could simply marvel at her magnificence.

The magnificence of her magical mane would be the envy of all the other folks on the planet. They became so envious and enraged that they created subtle laws to suppress the natural beauty of her hair. She would be scolded, chastised, harassed, and terminated from the most trivial employment positions simply because she chose to wear her hair naturally. She is the only female on the planet that is ostracized for wearing her hair naturally. Billions of dollars would be strategically invested to convince her that she is more beautiful if she wore her hair like all the other women on the planet who did not possess her magical, marvelous, magnificent mane. In their ignorance, they referred to her hair as `uncontrollable' as though being reluctant to submit to someone else's will was a bad thing.

That's was just the hair ladies and gentlemen, He hasn't created the mind, the Spirit, or the body as yet, **THAT WAS JUST THE HAIR ON HER HEAD**, and already she is the most magical creature on the planet, His melanin infused masterpiece. He made her more attractive than magnets, more striking than lighting. Her pleasing patterns were simply stunning. Her effect; enchanting. The most luminous stars in all the galaxies paled in comparison to the brilliance of the black woman. She had no business being so beautiful. She was so majestic in her might that it made absolute sense that every other race would invest billions in propaganda campaigns trying to convince her that she was anything but stunningly beautiful.

So of course, she is misunderstood, for indeed, she is a bold new look. Her flair is fetching, her effect, dazzling, a decorator's delight. She captured attention because she was conscious and curvy, cheerful and charming, cleverly coordinated, current, and cool. Her fluid style is flirtatious and feminine, fresh, and flawless. Blessed with a smile that could seduce both sinner and saint. One glance at her and the only thought that enters the mind is, 'What a mighty God we serve.'

Every other Being on Earth, for their mouth, God simply created a horizontal slit in their face and was like, 'Be off with you.' But for the black woman, he blessed her with big, bold, beautiful, luscious, delicious lips. Her lips were so dynamic that women of other races damn near depleted all the collagen on the planet, trying to copy what the black woman naturally owned with such regal grace. She is the embodiment of God's meticulous commitment to craftsmanship. She was beautifully finished and flawlessly rendered. Her ingredients were honey and cinnamon, enhanced with rich and harmonious materials. She is rare, exotic, and provocative. To say she was crafted by pure genius would be the ultimate understatement. She's the art of hand-tailored opulence, the epitome of elegance. She was a breakthrough in quality, the difference between nearly right and exactly right. Not to stare would be an insult to God Almighty Himself. Her natural beauty is undeniable; she is cocaine for the eyes, a symphony for the senses, a lavish display of defining details.

Thousands of women died every year, trying to duplicate her rear by surgical means. She raised a nation on the side of her hips. Her bountiful breasts nourished a nation of gods whose skin was as black as the vastness of the abyss but eyes bright as a thousand furnaces. The color of the nation that she birthed was the only color that was possible to witness the fiery brilliance of the stars, without such a color, no human would have any knowledge that stars existed. This was the magical color that God created her. To some degree, mere mortals were able to copy her shape in a lab, but the sway of her hips could not be duplicated because for that magic, God held the patent, the trademark, and the copyright.

A conversation with her is a celebration of the senses, a sensual feast, a delicious indulgence, dripping with polished perfection, a sweet sensation that is silky soft, smooth, and satisfying. She's a walking aphrodisiac. Behold God's ultimate creation. And for that reason, (among others) she is the most despised woman on the planet, she is by far the most envied. She is the most magical, yet the most molested, the most vivacious and the most violated. Yet her inner strength knows no boundaries because this woman was carefully crafted, delicately designed, unlike all others who were merely commanded into existence.

Her hips became a gateway for other gods to enter this mortal plane. She bore gods like Amun-Ra and Imhotep, Shango, Obatala, Osun, Isis and Osiris, Horus, and

Anubis. Warriors such as Hannibal, Shaka, Paul Bogle, Michael Manley, Bob Marley, Marcus Garvey, Malcolm, Nat Turner, and Nzinga. She gave birth to the Shona people, the Massai warriors, the Mali people, the Zulu tribe, the Abyssinian people, the Nubian people, the Somali nation. She birthed the scholars of Timbuktu, the wise men of Ethiopia. She gave birth to the Dogon tribe who a thousand years ago, knew more about the constellation than modern science knows today. She populated the Earth with cultural greatness, philosophers, mathematicians, astrologers, astronomers, scholars, and scientists. The greatest sculptures on the planet were carved by her sons and daughters, it was she who caused pyramids to manifest and left devils impressed. Her sons created the Sphinx and the Obelisk that Europeans later copied and called The Washington Monument. This melanin infused magical Being has no peer and no equal. Slavery was not her history; slavery interrupted her history. So put some respect on her name.

If Thinking About You.

If thinking about you were a crime,
Then convict me and take every dime.
Sentence me to maximum time,
Because woman, you stay on my mind.
Your ways how sweet, how tender,
Convict me now for I am a repeat offender.
Let not the Pope forgive me
Let the Governor condemn me,
Because the thought of you
Is embedded in my destiny.

Of your thought,
I have a lifetime subscription.
Should it be canceled,
Then bring me the lethal injection,
For your love is my affliction,
Your lips, my addiction.
Your kindness I could never forget,
Your beauty cannot be offset
So let the high court sentence me to death
For I haven't begun to love you yet.

If thinking about you took away from my poetry,
Then let me write no more.
Let me be as eloquent
As Mike Tyson on the Senate's floor.
Let mine be the novel that was never written,
For I am smitten.
There be none so majestic in all of Great Britain.
I want for nothing, for you are my all,
Your beauty be the reason cavemen chiseled on walls.
If Spring could be personified, it would have your face,
If the angels came to Earth, they would envy your grace.

To be with you,
There is nothing that I wouldn't do.
I would switch from Methodist to Baptist,
From capitalist to Communist,
From spoken word artist to vocalist
From team slam to soloist,
Whatever it took, woman so be it.
Because one kiss of your lips,
And I'm in heavenly bliss
Everything gets dismissed
As you become the emphasis.
My Revelation, my Genesis,
Woman, I fiend for this,

If I could no longer think of you,
Then let me not exist.

Extinguish my fire and send me
Into the Great Beyond,
If your touch no longer stimulates a response.
Let me rot in the jungles of the Amazon,
If our lips could no longer correspond.
Let the heavens realign the protons,
The neutrons and the electrons,
Let there be great destruction
From Pakistan to Oregon.
Let peace be gone,
And there be great phenomenons
If your face, I could no longer look upon.

Let my days be numbered
And my death be a slow one,
Let me follow the destruction of the Siren's song.
Let me break out in sores,
For which there are no cures
If for another, I should lust.
If I should betray your trust,
If for you, I should no longer make a fuss,
Then condemn me to the planet of Romulus,
And my fate, have the Klingons discuss.

Hang me from my esophagus,
For chasing an inferior stimulus
Leave me dangling and split me from the seam,
If I should gaze on anyone but my Black queen.

Heaven

Heaven is between the black woman's thighs,
If you've heard differently, you've been digesting lies.
You haven't seen true beauty
Until you look into those big brown eyes.
Until you kiss those luscious lips,
Then my son, you cannot testify.

Keep your Vogue magazine,
Your European platters can't tempt me,
Because even my enemies admit
That my woman be *Ironically Sexy*.
I leave them pissed
Because their women have that flat behind,
Agitated, because my woman is so goddamn fine.
Perturbed because the sun favors mine the most,
And in winter, my Jaquetta don't look like no ghost.
Winter, summer, fall, regardless of the season
Sisters be fine for no good goddamn reason.
If Heaven is between the black woman's thighs,
Then I am a sanctified saint,
For I have been to that Promised Land

That made me gave away all my earthly possessions Just
to say, "Fuck it, the landlord can wait."
I've been to that Promised Land
That gives new meaning to life. Left me sitting on
A rock in Tibet, Pondering,"How could
O.J trade in his Black wife?"

I don't want no implants, give me the real McCoy,
Because until you've been with a Black woman,
You don't know the meaning of *Almond Joy*.
All you've had is a sugar substitute.
You've been deceived from the days of your youth.
But as for me?
I live and die for my *Baby Ruth*.
Just to kiss and caress her *Butterfinger*
All night long, right into the break of day,
Climb her caramel *Mounds* and discover her *Milky Way*.

I pledge allegiance to the Black woman for I AM her man,
I would pay *100 Grand* just for a glimpse of her perfection.
Not for all the diamonds in the world,
The rubies and pearls,
Would you get me to forfeit
The sweetness of her *Whatchamacallit*.
The thing with the tight fit
The troubled soul repair kit,

The passion pit with a warmth that just won't quit,
The banana split that leaves me throwing fits.
It even made Mike Tyson gave away his championship.
I'm talking about that *Kit Kat* that feels like *Payday*,
The passageway that's off-*Broadway*
The sweet reward on display under the negligee,
That makes every day feels like Christmas,
Or better yet my birthday.
It is the utopia that I dream of when
It's time to get *Nutrageous*,
The great motivator that makes brothers courageous.
I would love to brag that,
"I'm strictly business when I'm all up in that good stuff."
But Lord knows I go coo coo for *Cocoa Puffs*.
Wrapped around my ebony chocolate like a *Twizzler*,
Have my *Twix* all up in her,
Her back arched and
Her body folds,
I felt her *Nestle Crunch* as she moved to the
Tootsie Roll. My lips encircled her *Mounds,* and our bodies
Gave off steam, A few more thrusts of the *Hershey Bar*
And I felt her cookie creamed.
As I double-dipped in her chocolate chip,
Betwixt her hips, my fudge got hot
And we were dripping with butterscotch.
She rocked my world,

As I worked her *Chocolate Swirl,*
Left me screaming, "You go girl."
Heaven is between the black woman's thighs,
And she's my only aphrodisiac.
If she were a crime, I would be a kleptomaniac,
If she were a sickness, I would be a hypochondriac.
Her fire burning with desire makes me a pyromaniac
Regardless of the circumstance, I take my coffee black.
She is that first ray of sunshine after a
Category 4 hurricane,
She is the word that Webster could not explain
The Demerol that eases my emotional pain,
The Queen that captures the King
In this mortal chess game.
Of the black woman
I have no complaints.
She's the reason I maintain,
Have me screaming Jesus' name.
She calls me, "Captain Kirk"
When I'm navigating her uncharted terrain.
She works me like a slave in the barnyard,
Makes me cum so hard
That the dresser, mirror, and headboard
Stood up and applaud.
Ebonicly speaking, the black woman is phat,
Between her thighs is where Heaven be at.

That cinnamon éclair,

That forces men to stare,

That brownie with the coffee latte,

Jamaican beef patty. That berry brown wheat toast,

West African gold coast,

Where I constantly overdose.

So if you have that Guinness Stout Stamina that won't die,

Combined with a cocoa butter brownie

That's the apple of your eye.

And she's willing to share with you

Her life time supply of pumpkin pie.

Allow you to sink in her fountain with your poetic pen,

Her caramel clutch releases all of your adrenaline,

As you become the patient and she becomes the RN.

Together you explode every now and then,

Making you want a white picket fence,

A dog and two children,

And the world seems like a better place to live in.

Then my son look no further,

You're in Heaven.

I Want To Write

Words transcend time,
They touch the souls
Of lives that haven't been conceived yet.
Our books will be read,
Our MP3s will be played long after our deaths.
So what does it profit a man
To gain the world and lose his soul?
I've seen wisdom in the youth
And fools that were damn near fifty years old.
I've seen poets prostitute their morals like
They were in a porno flick,
Racing to the stage just to suck their own dicks.
Egos get bruised, and poets fly into a rage
As if it were the norm.
On this stage, I've seen low self-esteem
Manifest itself in at least twenty different forms.

I've seen poets come to the stage with no substance,
Nothing but dramatic hype
Trying to convince us that my God,
And your God,

Hath commanded them to write.
I've seen poets wanting so badly to fit in,
Not being a part of "The big dawgs" is their greatest fear,
Grown men with kids, still falling victim
To pressures of their peers.
I've seen tens of thousands died innocently in Turkey,
I've sat back and watched
The Health Care System do us dirty.
Overzealous cops waiting to serve me,
Politicians lined up to jerk me.
I've seen souls die,
When all they needed
Was one encouraging word
To make them feel worthy.
But still, I see poets coming to the stage
All puffed up like they're royalty.
Wanting the world to bow to them
Because they wrote some poetry.

I've seen poets names
Unintentionally left off of a flyer,
And for weeks, they remain vexed.
In this game, I've seen big egos come
With even bigger inferiority complex.
I've seen poets rush to the stage
To deliver nothing but low blows.

Small men enslaved by big egos,
Led astray by their amigos,
Idiots looking up to imbeciles
As though they were heroes.

I've seen poets been in this game for years,
And has yet to lift one soul higher,
But let them tell it,
You'll swear to God
You've met the Messiah.
Blockheads dripping with counter-productiveness,
Feeblemindedness, idiotic, moronic,
And unconsciousness.
A literary reject,
With a compromised intellect.
Joker comes on stage,
Unprofound like that,
But swear that egotistical bullshit was phat.
Never a kind word to leave their mouth,
Some poets be ugly from the inside out.
But I ignore them when they roll up
Week after week after week,
Because the more attention
That you give low self-esteem,
The more it seeks.

I've seen poets write with only one goal,
And that is to pull down their neighbor.
Dying to be an icon,
Because someone taught them
How to mate a pen
With a clean sheet of paper.
Like I've said,
I've seen grown men with childish behaviors.

I've seen poets attempt to glorify
Their gift to the entire nation,
As if self-praise is some
Sort of recommendation.
Hypocrites come on stage with masks,
Trying to deceive you and me,
Poor fools don't know that
Their wicked ways speak
Volumes louder than their poetry.

And as sure as day will eventually turn to night
Poets will continue to turn knives in backs,
And mics they'll jack,
For two seconds more under the spotlight.
Convinced that being an ass is their birthright,
Quick to talk about their third eye, yet they lack insight.
Running to the mic only to feed their egotistical appetite,

But what's the use of being a poet
If you're not gonna touch one soul tonight?
What's the use of being a poet,
If you're going to make us regret
That we stayed to hear you on this open mic?
What's the use of being a poet,
If you're not going to make a difference?
If your entire agenda is built on
Burning bridges and constructing fences?
If you only write to impress groupies,
And start beefs that are senseless?

You need to chill with your material,
Revise it and spend more time,
Because that bullshit you come on stage with
Is nothing but the idiotic
Ranting of an inferior mind.

But while poets continue
To blow each other apart like dynamite
I want to write.
I want to change lives.
I want to touch somebody deep down inside.
I want to give that homeless mother new reasons to cope.
Let mine be the voice that encourages
That child that was born addicted to dope.

I want to write the words
That made me hold on while Sickle Cells
Found new and improved ways to rip through my bones.
A fever that wouldn't check, swollen joints,
But inadequate insurance,
So doctors weren't trying to hear me moan.

I want to give that HIV positive child
New reasons to hold on.
I want to write the words that make racists
Look upon themselves with scorn.
Shine light on date rape in college dorms.
Let me reach that neglected child
Who thought he was better off dead.
Let me write the words that need to be said.
I want to write from that deep,
Dark, dirty, disgusting place
That little girls retreat to when daddy
Secretly climbs in their bed.

Let my words regenerate, rejuvenate and revitalize,
Restore hope, restore health, and breathe new life.
Let me write the words
To bring about an exemption from hostilities,
Give rebirth to liberty and tranquility,
Civility and chivalry.

That old fashion courtesy,
That keyboard harmony,
That long lost gallantry.

From this stage, I want to scream
The words that the world refuses to hear,
The so-called 'Unpopular Truth.'
Rip open my chest cavity
And share with you the scars of my youth.
Unveil this mask and show
You the real face of child abuse.
Let me write the words
That causes the unproductive to produce,
Cultivate the uncultivated, and polish the rude.
Let me cause the unaccomplished to
Implement, terminate, execute,
Dispatch and conclude.
Make the most hard-core Jamaican
Stand back and say,
"Gwaaan, my youth!"

If words can heal, then let me write the words
To remove hatred from at least one face.
Forget black and white,
I want to write the poem that heals
And uplift the entire human race.

Take that junkie to that higher place,
Transcend time, energy, and space.

But I refuse to be another poet
Who spits arrogance in your face.
So while others have egos to build
And inferiority complexes to fight,
Until the day I die,
I've got poems to write.

A Prayer for Social Media

Lord grant me self esteem so adequate that I am able to keep my minor accomplishments the fuck off of social media. Help me to love myself enough so I that I will not feel the need to post ten selfies per day in the hopes that I will eventually feel worthy because nine strangers liked one of my highly filtered pictures.

Beloved baby Jesus from Bethlehem, please rebuke the need out of me to post every goddamn meal that you've ever provided. There's no need for me to act as if my life is more fabulous than it is because I'm at Cheesecake Factory charging a meal at 29% interest on my $300 limit credit card, which is the maximum credit that my 550 score allows me.

Lord, you know these bills keep a bitch grounded, so please help me release the need to post my airport location the two times per year that I get to hop on these cheap-ass domestic Frontier airlines flights. By now my followers should know what the fuck an airport looks like, I really don't need to post pictures of me waiting to board, but I can't help it. It makes a bitch feel relevant and accomplished. You can understand that, can't you Lord?

Oh, merciful Father, please do not make the thousands of followers who worship me, privy to the reason why I get on a social media platform and argue with total strangers for disagreeing with my perspective is because of how empty my pathetic little life is.

If you could just keep that secret between us, Father, don't let them peep that shit Lord, don't let them peep that shit.

Oh loving God, I'm 42 years old and just became a vegan three days ago, help me find the words to scorn and shame these filthy consumers of flesh, these spiritual savages, these sick sons of psychopathic bitches. Help me select the correct hashtag that will let them know in no uncertain terms that I am better and nobler than they could ever hope to be. Allow me the spiritual arrogance to correctly belittle these low vibrational beings Lord. If you're not embracing an alkaline lifestyle then I can't fuck with your low frequency, blocked chakra, spiritually compromised ass. Hashtag: Plant-based lifestyle bitches. Greta Thunberg was right.

Dear Virgin Mary, Mother Of God, and all the patron saints who hear my humble plea, I beseech thee, please, whenever I post one of my selfies with the duck lips and excessive cleavage, then proceed to place a Paramashansa Yogananda quote beneath it so that I can appear profound, (or any other Indian guru with an existential quote that only a motherfucker who shops at LuLu Lemon and buys fresh squeezed tangerine juice from Trader Joe's would be able to decipher) please for God's sake and little baby Jesus' I am begging you, don't let my followers see through that shallow shit and realize that I am about as deep as a goddamn puddle. I was educated in the United States public school system Lord, you know, intelligence ain't my strong suit. Up until last week, I thought melancholy was a seasonal fruit. Please don't let my followers realize that my sense of self is so terribly inadequate that I get on these social media platforms begging for validation from people who I have never met and most likely will never meet.

Oh, precious Lord and Savior, my blessed Redeemer, Jehovah Jireh, my provider, your grace is sufficient for me. I'm asking you to please place a watchful eye over my hand and have me stop typing stupid shit saying that I am sending thoughts and prayers to everyone who is allegedly facing some challenges in their lives. You know as well as I do that I don't give a fuck about these strangers Lord. I only do that shit to sound more spiritual and compassionate. Thank you Father for hearing and answering my prayers. Peace and blessings y'all, much Love and Light. Sending ascension energies to all my beloveds. Hashtag: Namaste bitches.

Please Jesus, whenever I post these pics of my Gucci this, and my Versace that, and my Loui this, and my designer that, and my late model this, and my red bottom that, please don't have any of these haters misinterpret these blessed posts as unhealed trauma seeking attention and validation. Folks with real understanding of wealth invest in assets, I prefer to forge my own path and diversify heavily in liabilities. So have these bitches understand that I am successful Lord, through your grace and divine mercies, of course. But for the grace of God, there goes I, won't He do it? Child, won't he do it? Look at God; just look at God.

Oh, precious Lord, Father God, Jehovah Jireh, El Shaddai, Elohim Most Exalted Savior Of Humanity, I'm in my mid-forties Lord, and you know for my entire life a bitch done shied away from any sort of personal development, introspection, personal accountability, and spiritual growth, so as expected human beings don't really fuck with my highly sensitive, unreasonable, irrational ass no more Lord. Over the years, they just kinda let a bitch be. No worries, I've adopted this cute little dog from a shelter, and as you can see Lord, I've dressed the little motherfucker up in a brightly colored wool hat and matching sweater, and I engage it in one-sided conversations like it's a goddamn human being. No Lord, I'm not losing my mind, he actually loves it, (isn't that right my sweet little snucums.) Mommy loves you, smooches. It's the only male energy I have in my life Lord. Through this fulfilling relationship, I'm allowed to receive unconditional love without learning a goddamn thing about loving unconditionally. I call it a win/win Lord. I love dogs more than people, they never stay mad at you, and you never have to learn how to apologize or be accountable for any of your actions. Isn't that precious? Lord, The Law of Diminishing Dick states that as the frequency of dick diminishes from my life, the more human traits and characteristics I will project unto the dog. It's not only happening Lord, but it has also happened! Shit is real. Help me Jesus!

Ok, this is Empty Shell signing off. P.S. Lord don't let the good folks who are envying my fabulous life on social media peep the fact that I would trade this fucking mutt for a real man in a minute if only one would tolerate my exceptionally toxic ass. Hashtag dog lovers unite. Dog lovers are better than those crazy cat people.

I invested a couple of dollars in Bitcoin last year Lord, a couple months ago I watched a few YouTube videos, now

I'm Forex trading up in this bitch, fucking with commodities and futures and shit. Buy low, sell high, straight Wall Street type of shit. Father God, have these fools recognize that I'm a certified day trader and investment guru life coach, and I am by no means trying to appear more successful than I am. So what if I lost all my shit in that 2020 Corona Virus stock market plummet. (Hashtag cryptocurrency bitches.) BTW if you need your credit repaired, type info in the comments. I got you.

I pray the continued blessing of sweet baby Jesus upon this Facebook platform, Twitter and Instagram Father God, continue to cause an increase in my number of followers Father God, an increase in my comments and likes Father God, bless each and every one of these blessed posts Father God with likes and comments Father God, and if you could have a couple of celebrities retweet some of my posts Father God, that would be fucking amazing Father God. I pray all these blessings and more in Jesus' precious name, thy will be done ect, ect, hashtag follow me bitches but a bitch don't follow back.

Amen.

Conversation with Success

I observed my people, maintaining that all is well,
When indeed, we're wretched.
We strut around, clothed in fear
As we constantly yield to despair.
Why is this life so abusive?
Wealth so reclusive?
And Success so elusive?
I needed some answers, and I cared not to wait
My questions were simply legit
So I decided to pay Success a visit.

Snuck up on him like a medieval lancer,
Focused, like Tina Turner in Private Dancer
Before he knew it, I was on that ass like colon cancer.
Flashed the MAC 10 equipped with and silencer
Homeboy tonight you gonna give me some answers.

What's the deal between you and my people?
Yo son, you done dissed us
It's obvious that you blacklisted us
We don't see you come Christmas?

Look at you...
Enjoying the surplus, living stupendous,
While we're walking around self-conscious.
And even if you do allow us to hit the lotto, that's a joke
Because within five years, we're back to being broke.
And the majority of my people are beginning to lose hope.
So I'm fitting to break you down like an improper fraction
Cause when it comes to my people,
Yo son, you're missing in action.

Success looked at me with disappointment.
He said, "Kirk is that a gun?
Violence? Is that how you solve your problems?"
He said, "Man you're the one that's a joke
Put the gun away, cause ain't nobody getting smoked"
Besides, what you just said, you don't actually believe it
In fact, your body language reveals it.
You're just trying to write some controversial poetry
Because had you believe that, you would've never found
me.

He said, "Kirk Nugent I AM Success,
I've been around before any of these planets were evident
I've been around from before
The whole Adam and Eve incident
And I've yet to meet someone

Who has met me by accident.
If you want to see me,
You're going to have to be far more than diligent.
Kirk Nugent, you're going to have to be
Intoxicated with the wine of persistence.
You're going to have to step
To your fears like they were irrelevant
Son, you're going to have to
Step with so much confidence
That providence takes precedence
Not before then, will I ever enter your residence.
So tell your people that they can never
See me sitting in front of BET."

I'm not here to scold you, but I told you,
Look for me on the shelves of Barnes and Noble.
Seek me diligently even when you're most distressed
Because with your excuses, I refuse to be impressed.
You'll find me between the pages
Unlocking the wisdom of the ages
Sharing ideas with modern-day sages of all races.
Yet you have the nerve to imply that I'm a racist.

Now if I'm a racist then please explain to me
How do you account for a Bob Marley,
Or is he just an anomaly?

What about Marcus Garvey,
Phillis Wheatley and Booker T
John H. Johnson, who founded Jet and Ebony?
Dick Gregory. Alex Haley, Pearl Bailey,
Bayard Rustin, and Dr. King.
Billie Holiday, Cab Calloway.
How do you explain Jesse, Owens, not Jackson!
Toni, Morrison, and Braxton?
Sugar Ray and Jackie Robinson.
What about the great Hannibal who fought bitterly?
Or the Moors who conquered Italy?
Michael Eric Dyson, Tyson,
I said, 'Tyson?'
He said, 'Yeah, Beckford, Mike, and Cicely.
The Matrix developed a glitch in that bitch
Trying to figure out what to do with Kappernick.
What about Jigga man who packs the arenas,
Your girls, Venus and Serena,
Miss Misdemeanor,
Forget about Ike; let's talk about Tina.
Lauren Hill and Beyonce who killed it later,
Will and Jada
Come on Kirk, don't make me dis' ya
By now, you should've gotten the picture.
I said, "Word son, I'm with cha."

He said, "The fact of the matter is,
This has little to do with race
But has everything to do with the distribution
Of time, energy, and space."
Mismanage any of those three,
And your failure is imperative
That's why according to the
Social Security Administration
At age sixty-five,
45% of Americans are still dependent on relatives
30% must live on charity;
In other words, with me, there is no familiarity.
23% are still working,
Basically, they're barely maintaining
Only 2% are self-sustaining.
So in actuality, after forty years of toil
On a job that they deliberately signed up
Financially speaking, 98% of Americans
Could not pick me out of a police line up.

They complain as they struggle to
Keep abreast of the mortgage,
That the reason they call it the American dream is
Because you have to be asleep to believe that garbage.
But they lack the courage to believe that
They have the capacity to make it

Not knowing that the most talented,
Is often overtaken by the most dedicated.
So they fake it, and by default,
Their misfortune, they create it, orchestrate it.
Most live their lives hiding behind precautions
Then somewhere in their early forties,
They come to me with that emotional extortion.

That, 'Somebody done me wrong' song.
That, 'Poor little me, I've been struggling for oh so long.'
Emotionally they'll try to choke you,
But remember I told you
Discipline is what separates
The magnificent from the mediocre.

My name is Success; I'm there for all who seek
But you don't get to me by watching
Twenty-nine hours of television per week.
Your dreams are not there for you to diminish,
You've got to be in it to win it
So if there's something that you seek,
Then by God, begin it.
But most people go around finding fault
Like there's a reward in it.
Kirk, I'm sick of it.
It's ridiculous.

Crippled by their inertia, they turn around and blame fate,
Not knowing that you don't have to
Be great to get started,
But you have to get started in order to be great.
I find it extremely odd,
How their chances of success,
They continue to rob.
In fact, most people stop looking for work
Once they've found a job.
Ask the ones who complain the most,
Letting off the most steam
In the past 90 days, how much time have they spent
Actively working on their dreams?
What books have they read?
What seminars have they attended
To move them closer to their objectives?
Ask them Kirk, and you'll see the
Answer is always negative.

To sit at my footstool, that begins with a choice.
So today be certain what you choose,
Because excuses don't explain,
And explanations don't excuse.
And I don't have time for all these victims
Complaining to me about the system

When the door to my office is opened with self-discipline.

He said, "To see me, you're going to have to
Inhale your fears like they were medicinal,
Your dedication better be phenomenal
Because you're going to need
More conviction than a career criminal."
Come out here with both guns cocked like an outlaw
Bring that passion; son give it to me raw,
You do that, and I'll support you like a Wonderbra.
Transform you from average to Avatar,
From Kool-Aid to caviar,
Remove your battle scars and make you a superstar
Resurrect your life like my name was Amen-Ra.
Anything less,
I'm gonna treat you like you're soft,
Shut you down like Vicks vapor rub on a bad cough
If you can't bring me the passion
Then homeboy step off.

So stay true to your divinity, seek to go beyond infinity
Then persistence and discipline will become your savior.
But excuses will derail you, financially jail you,
Because excuses are the nails that
Are used to build the house of failure.
Of the perpetual victim, too many

People have become the epitome,
The fact of the matter is we've become our worst enemy
So tell your people that they will never see the best of me
Until they stop confusing bad management with destiny.

You Deserve Better

It has been estimated that there are over
50 trillion cells in the human body
That's trillion with a T.
And it has been further proven that
Each of those cells has within it consciousness.
In other words, intelligence.
Intelligence that our most
Supercalifragilisticexpialidocious
Awesome computer cannot duplicate.
I said **CANNOT** duplicate.

Now please allow me to put this into perspective.
Because we've designed a computer;
And in charge of this computer,
In a remote office in Virginia, sits a man.
And this man can pilot an
Unmanned vehicle in Afghanistan.
And out of a population of millions,
He can target one individual.
One individual who does not look like him,
Does not dress like him,

Does not pray like him,
And does not believe like him.

And with one decision,
He can eradicate that man
With such precision,
In the fields of Afghanistan,
That the body would be dead before it hits the ground.
And he can then leave his office with enough time,
To be back home with no strife,
To sit and watch the current episode
Of Scandal with his wife.
Because Olivia Pope has never been this dope,
And as long as it's not your scandal
That's being brought to light
Or you and your spouse had a fight,
Then you'll pretty much sleep all right tonight.
Yet that billion dollar supercomputer,
And that multi-million-dollar drone
Is garbage compared to the intelligence
Found in one of your cells.
And we have over 50 trillion
Of those cells in our body.
So my question is, "Is this it?"

As intelligent a Being as you are,

The life that you are living;
Is that the best life that
You can design for yourself?
Is this it?
Is this the best that we can do?
And if we should be honest with ourselves
Then the answer would be a resounding no,
To just about everything that we do.
So my question is, "What's stopping you?"

What's stopping you from
No longer getting up at the crack of dawn
To hurry and get dressed
To sit in bumper to bumper traffic?
Just to get to a job that is stressing you,
To serve a boss who doesn't appreciate you,
Who sees no value in you.
And forget that your stomach
Is trying to get you out of your seat,
But this boss assigns you the time of day
That you are allowed to eat.
And even though you're a grown adult
Who doesn't believe in mind-games,
Nor do you indulge in tricks,
But if you're out for more than two days,
Then you better prove that you were sick.

Now you're deep in debt, so you're praying,
"Lord, have mercy."
Because you fought adversity
In New Jersey to graduate that University.
And a degree called a Masters is what they gave,
Because you bought into the idea that the road to
The American Dream, this degree will pave.
But here you are, ten years later
With a 'Masters' and you're still a slave.
And every day your joy is getting
Just a little bit harder to summon
Because you know ain't no proclamation coming.
And you can feel breathing down your neck,
The breath of fear,
Because this dream is beginning
To look like the American nightmare.

And if you think about climbing
That corporate ladder,
My brother, don't even bother.
Not the way they pit you
Against each other.
Your coworker?
Oh, you're going to have to jerk her.
She's simply a necessary adversary

Smiling in your face,
And sometimes you have to skin a few cats
For a piece of cheese in this rat race.

But thank God for saving grace,
Today you're putting in your request
Six months in advance,
Without leaving your assigned station.
Looking forward to that one week off
To take the family on vacation.
But keeping up with the bills doesn't afford you
The sensation of traveling
Across this abundant nation.
So just like last year,
Once again, you're doing a STAYcation.

You're staying at home,
Damn near depressed.
But no time to think about that,
Got get back to your desk
Because they keep you pressed.
Your health is deteriorating
From the stress
But oh yes, TGIF.
So you rush to your car
Hoping to do Happy Hour at the bar.

But instead, you're back to doing the
Bumper to bumper thing my dear,
And just like that traffic,
Your life is going nowhere.

And you long for all
The beauty of life to be showered,
If only you were born into
A network that's empowered.
But if you want to be something
That you've never been
Then today, you're going to have to
Do something that you've never done.

So how long are you going to remain cautious
To the point of being nauseous?
What will it take for you to get off
The hamster wheel of this nation?
What will it take for you to transcend
Maslow's Hierarchy of Needs
From security to self-actualization?
You are by no means powerless,
So I am asking you not to
Just sit there and fret.
How long are you going
To tiptoe through life

Hoping to arrive safely at death?

You were created by Divine Source
And Infinite Intelligence it gave,
Freedom is your birthright
From the cradle to the grave.
So believe me when I tell you that
**YOU DID NOT COME HERE
TO BE NO SLAVE!**
No slave to no job,
No slave to no bills,
No slave to no student loans,
No slave to no credit score,
That is not what you were created for.

And there is someone out there
Who is coming from a much darker place
Than you have ever seen
And believe me when I tell you
That today, she's living her dreams.
So it doesn't matter who you are
And what you do,
I'm saying that dream in your heart
It is possible for you.

So look at your gifts and begin to take stock

Because in order to make this leap,
You're not only going to have to think,
You're going to have to act outside of the box.
But you think that if you don't have a job,
Then you're done.
I'm asking you please,
Stop beating that drum.
In today's economy,
You don't need a job,
You need an income.

And life will grind you
To a pulp, if you let her,
But she will yield to your desires
If with conviction you tell her,
That, 'I deserve better!'
So send this life of mediocrity
And compromise back to the kitchen,
You're now creating from
A consciousness that is much broader
This nonsense is not what you ordered.
And I know as pathetic as it sounds,
Your ego would rather me not say this,
But have you save face
And continue to live in fear.
However, it is your best thinking

That has brought you here.

So if there are some new skills
That you need to acquire
Then by God, go ahead and get 'em.
If there are some books that you need to read,
Then listen when someone suggests them.
And if someone has created
Some training on the internet
Then God bless 'em.
And if you have to step
Outside of your comfort zone,
Then start stepping,
But be open to the lessons.
Be willing to look
At opportunities with new eyes
And stop blocking your blessings.

This is what I know to be true,
The dream that is possible for me
Is also possible for you.
So I am asking you;
I am asking you today
To commit to the life
That you've always adored.
I am asking you today,

To walk away from mediocrity
And slam the door.
I am asking you today,
To step out on the playing field of life,
With the intention to score.
And it is not over until
You walk away with your dreams;
No, not a moment before.
So basically I'm asking you today
To decide to be a slave no more.

My Past (Intro)

Love has evaded me
Escaped me,
Now, this loneliness plagues me.
When I was younger, with love, I was not concerned.
My only focus was maintaining my groove,
I had that boxer's philosophy,
"Stick and move, stick and move."

I kept my heart tucked away,
Buried deep within the soul,
My only prerequisite, a pulse, and a hole.
No doubt, I was cold.
Women in retrospect that I should've made my wife,
I found ingenious ways to sweep them out of my life.
Their tears flowed willingly,
As my illogical actions drove them insane,
And it seems as if, somewhere in my psyche,
I've cross-reference love and pain.

I came from a childhood
Where love was never expressed,
My parents stayed stressed, vexed.

At best they tolerated each other,
And the kids were a mere financial bother.
I felt like I survived an abortion,
Or committed some deadly sin,
And family didn't seem like something
That I needed to be in.
Sickle Cell kept playing games with me,
Over and over again.
It would bring me to death's door,
But wouldn't completely drag me in.
It would show me all the splendor of death,
The great escape
And I prayed it would take me in.
Instead, it returned me to
This dysfunctional family which
I was forced to live in.

In my teenage years, I overheard my mom saying,
"There is no such thing as a good man."
And with glee, my twenty-year-old sister agreed.
It was then I made the decision,
That I'll be damned if one of these bitches use me,
Abuse me, refuse me,
As long as I live, I'm gonna do me.

By the time I got on the dating scene,
My heart was encased in steel walls.

I gave whatever compliment and
Conversation they needed,
In short, I would talk my way to the draws.
I would enter loving relationships,
Thinking all problems solved,
The only problem is,
My emotions would never get involved.
I've walked away from women
Who were perfect for me,
Left them pondering,
"What went wrong?"
"I can't even believe this!"
But, how could a grown man tell a woman
That his childhood broke him?
And at twenty-two, he was still picking up the pieces.
Demons playing back voices inside my head,
The first two people I loved,
Returned my love by saying,
"I wish you were dead."

So I walk away,
Trying not to feel guilty,
Fearing if I love you, you won't love me back,
And woman, that would just kill me.
Baby, I'm losing this battle against love fast,
Isn't it obvious?
My Past Keeps Kicking My Ass.

My Past Keeps Kicking My Ass

They say that a cow never knows
The use of its tail until he loses it,
And a fool once he finds love,
Sure as hell abuses it.
Well, I be that fool, and I am that cow,
Because someway, somehow
I find "New and improved" ways
To destroy the love that we've built.
Before you know it, I'm off to the next, "Vic."
Leave you standing with the guilt.
I have you thinking that it was something you said
Or maybe even the things that you do,
When in fact, a fool like me
Doesn't deserve to be loved by you.

Coming from a past that I can't seem to get over,
And these demons standing in the way
Won't allow us to get closer.
My Past Keeps Kicking My Ass
And these demons won't let me go,
I keep reaching for your love

And my past be like,
"Oh, hell no."
And I can't remember when this psychosis started,
But check the DNA of my soul
And you'll find fibers of a broken heart.
Baby, I'm coming from a past
Filled with just too many sorrows,
My demons saw you coming
And they snatched Cupid's arrows.

My Past Keeps Kicking My Ass
And these demons won't let me be,
Won't let you get close to me.
I pray thee, forgive me,
For changing the course of destiny,
Because I know that you are feeling me.
And I am on bending knees,
With God, I plead,
Please release me
And let these demons set me free,
Because we were meant to be.

I've been a loner all my life.
Word! I wasn't looking for no wife,
Or someone to make me feel all warm inside,
Rob me of my foolish pride.

Then you said whenever you're alone
You can smell my cologne.
And I'm thinking, "Damn baby, how true."
Because everything reminds me of you,
Or us two,
And the silly things that we do.
Across a crowded room, you catch my stare,
And you know I'm thinking,
I wish these people would just disappear
I swear, I want you here, near.
But my demons are filled with fear.
They're protecting my heart,
About yours, they don't care.
They'll do more to avoid pain
Than to gain any pleasure,
So they always find a way to bury my treasure.

As I take my hand and wipe the tears from your eyes,
Because I have no tissue,
I ask, "Why God?
Why did I have to come with so many issues?
Why must my past dictate my future?
This woman loves me, but you insist that I lose her."
Our attraction runs far more than the physical,
She moves me on levels far deeper than the spiritual.
She has eyes for no one but me,

And at first, I thought it was the bald head,
The goatee, maybe even the poetry.
But it was on a deeper level that she was feeling me.

Her eyes have that divine honesty,
She possessed such modesty,
But subconsciously,
I don't think that I deserve you,
So I find new and improved ways to jerk you,
Unnerve you.
Determined not to let YOU and I become WE
But you find new and improved ways to forgive me,
Which leaves me feeling more and more unworthy.

So even though you are here
And I'm feeling you the most,
My past warns not to let you get close.
It questions your every move,
Measure your quality time by the ounce.
It shelters my emotions
So it wouldn't even matter if you decided to bounce.
And you asked, "How could I be so callous?"
When deep down, you know that I care.
But I swear, the real question is my dear,
Can you, who are motivated by love,
Reform me, who is motivated by fear?

My Past Keeps Kicking My Ass
And these demons won't let me go,
Saying, you're a friend now,
But sooner or later you'll be a foe.
Making general comparisons,
Showing me all there is to fear,
My past won't allow me to focus
On your beauty growing here.

And baby I have nothing, nothing but regrets,
Damn near three decades
And I still haven't learned how to love yet.
As I search the crevices of my mind,
Wondering why all my relationships
Seem like I'm doing time,
And it's only after I destroy the beauty
That I had with you,
Where I stop and think,
"Oh shit, Déjà vu."

I'm tired, tired of all this hurting,
Perfect relationship, six months later,
It ain't working.
You tell me that love conquers all,
But it was the abuse of love that built these walls,

So no longer do I give my all.
'Cause when you step, I have nothing left.
Forget what you've been told,
Emotionally I'm cold
There are only burnt bridges to my soul.
So even though you feel so right
And you make me feel so whole,
To get you out of my life is the subconscious goal.
Yeah, you make me feel complete,
When I'm with you
The world becomes an oyster at my feet.
But my past keeps looking for deceit
Keeps telling me sooner or later you'll creep,
Sooner or later, you'll trample my heart under your feet.
So in fear, I retreat without being discreet,
And once again, my life becomes bittersweet.

My Past Keeps Kicking My Ass,
And baby it ain't fair to you,
Wondering where we went wrong;
You ain't got a clue,
Because I keep feeding you
From a past menu
Residues of old rendezvous,
That I can't seem to undo.
And there's only so much that you can deal with,

It's just a matter of time before you get tired
Of my bullshit.
You gave me love, and I abused it,
But this destiny, baby, I didn't choose it.
I hope you find the courage to forgive me,
I swear, my intentions were not to hurt thee.
My actions I cannot condone,
And it seems like I am destined to be alone.
At least that's what you said
As you walked through the door,
You told me that my relationships would never last,
Until I find a way
To kick my past in the ass.

I Need You to Remember

I've been three decades in the darkness,
Three decades in the wilderness
Three decades of amnesia,
And now I'm beginning to remember.
I know that you're thinking that we haven't met
Don't get too perplexed, but hear me before you step
When I say, "My God, you look familiar!"
I am beginning to remember that we're born of Light
Created to shine long before infinity could tell time,
And we cannot be denied.

So now, I am beginning to shed this programming.
I am beginning to realize that these people that I hate
I don't really know them,
But it's the patriotic thing to do.
So now I am beginning to move away from
MANipulation Towards self-actualization,
Towards wisdom and inner peace.
And the turbulence cease like an absence of the breeze
And I'm beginning to like this energy.
I am beginning to realize that there is
No separation between God and me

So now, I am beginning to be like the tree.

For no tree has branches
So foolish as to fight among themselves,
And we're all branches of the same tree called humanity.
And I need you to remember.
Now I'm beginning to straighten my back,
Raise up off my knees,
My connection to sun, moon, and star

Get decreed, like I was Cherokee Recognizing his
Oneness to spirit Outside of his tepee,
And for the first time in my life,
I am free.

How could I've been so shallow?
As to wage war against my shadow.
Born of the same spirit, just different faces
But now I'm beginning to remember that
The fight is not against flesh and blood
But spiritual wickedness in high and low places.
I am beginning to remember that free will
Cannot be bought,
I'm a member of the Ground Crew sent to
Stop the onslaught.

So no longer shall I major in victimology
Opposed to opportunity,
Not when I was born with the winning credentials,
A spirit that's celestial.

So today, I'm like a team of Army Rangers
Cause even though we're so-called strangers,
Not one soul gets left behind.
So the question is
Can these bones live?
And without a shadow of a doubt
I assure you that the answer
Is `Affirmative!`

Oh ye of little faith,
You were born to win Destined to be great.
What comfort do you find
In these aches and pain?
Why do you endorse the crying game?
Why do you deny that
You're a reflection of the Most High?
And why do you allow yourself
To be manipulated into shame?
Come on think,
It is important that you remember.

For everything in our lives, we're responsible.
So my dear friend, is it possible,
That the reason we're dissatisfied with our conditions
Impatient with our solutions,
Is because we've been asking the wrong questions?
Those who dance are considered insane
By those who can't hear the music.
And volunteer victims soon grow sick
Of a life that's all too basic.
You are Light vibrating consciousness
So why do you choose to cooperate with this wickedness?
Why live your lives trying to please human beings
Who knows nothing about being human?
Because if they did, it would be understood
That the true meaning of compassion,
Is without ridicule, allowing a man to pursue his passion.
Without tyranny affording a woman the opportunity
To manifest her destiny.

To dream the impossible dream
To shoot for the moon and live among the stars.
Within the questions lie the answers
To all the concerns of your heart.

And it is critically important
That you find peace, Long before you're deceased.

So forgive my intrusion, this mental fender bender
But now more than ever, I need you to remember.
They've rolled the dice so now your life is at stake
Whether you ride or die depends on your ability to
Stay awake, AKA your emotional maturity.
But without the questions,
Ladies, and gentlemen, there can be no clarity.

I'm talking about a commitment to total responsibility. A
lack thereof places your life in jeopardy.
But unlike Alex Trebek, today I'm giving you the
Questions. Hopefully, they'll cut through the upholstery
Penetrate deep into the extrasensory
Like a brain on a treadmill,
I'm trying to jog your memory
So help me help you
To escape this penitentiary.
First question is:
Who's in charge of your destiny?
Can someone actually MAKE you mad
Or did you choose to linger in resentment?
Are you loving everything that you do,
Or is this the life that your parents prescribed for you?
Your job; is that your passion
Being manifested on the physical scene
Or are you just building someone else's dream?

I hope I didn't lose you
But within the answers to those questions
Lie the direct quality of your future,
So it is important that you remember.

Do you really believe that
Someone else can complete you?
Are there any human beings above or beneath you?
Who besides yourself can break your heart?
Victor or victim, who chooses your path?
Everything is a choice, are you aware of that as yet?
And would you be mad at me if I told you that
No one can make you angry; you chose to be upset.
The challenges of life are here to make us better, not bitter.
Did you realize that everyone you encounter in
Life is your teacher?
To balance the equation, you become their teacher in turn
And the lesson repeats until the lesson is learned.

So who's in charge of your happiness?
Your loneliness, your emptiness?
Most of your worries are senseless
And someone else's opinion of you
Is none of your business.

Why do you choose to sing along with the given chorus?
What gives your life purpose?

When did you become so pacified
And what will it take for you to be satisfied?

Do you know how much I love you?
Of course not, can't tell you that,
What if you don't love me back?
I would rather wait until you're lying in a mahogany box
Such a paradox.
But isn't that how the script is usually read?
So the question is,
Do you honor the living
As passionately as you mourn the dead?

Remember when you would leap
And grow your wings on the way down?
What happened to that?
Remember when you used to live in the moment?
Of course not?
You were only two then,
And since then, you were trained to repress who you are,
Your sense of adventure.
But this poem wouldn't be so long
If it wasn't important
That you remember.

When was the last time you did

Something for the first time?
Better yet, how much quiet time do you
Set aside deprogram your mind?
Remove the blindfold and behold
You're so much more
Than you've been told.
You're like an emperor
Who chooses to panhandle.
Like the sun believing
It were a mere candle.
You were born blessed, never cursed
Yet you behave like the
Ocean dying of thirst.

But I can feel your spirit now,
You're tired; you want to put an end
To all this illusion,
Delusion and confusion,
You want the chaos to cease.
You just want peace.

So now you can no longer ignore
That voice in your core
Telling you that this life,
It just has to be about something more. And just like you,
I don't want any enemies.
I want to sit in the presence

Of a loving family,
One called humanity,
Dipped in spirituality,
Where there's a sense
Of sensibility.
But they're feeding us complexities Stereotypes and
Warlike theories. And we are oblivious of the fact that
Mentally we're chained in slavery.
How could we be so blind?
This is the question that frustrates me.

But I guarantee you this,
If today we should refrain
From spiritual suicide,
Starve the ego until it is deceased.
Then tonight,
The genocide would cease.
Because just like it requires
Billions of pebbles
For a mountain to be
Constructed with ease.
So is world peace constructed by
Billions of souls with inner peace.
Now, do you understand why
It is important that you remember?

Made in the USA
San Bernardino, CA
08 April 2020